Booth !
#6119

$4 50

W9-AZF-960

TX 4-547-215

TX0004547215

The Sandlot Game

❧

An Anthology of
Baseball Writings

❧

Edited by Dick Wimmer

mp
MASTERS / PRESS

A Division of Howard W. Sams & Company

Published by Masters Press
A Division of Howard W. Sams & Company
2647 Waterfront Pkwy E. Dr, Suite 100,
Indianapolis, IN 46214

Library of Congress Cataloging-in-Publication Data
The sandlot game / edited by Dick Wimmer.
       p.   cm.
   ISBN 1-57028-120-3 (cloth)
   1. Baseball -- United States. 2. Baseball players -- United
States -- Biography. 3. Baseball stories. I. Wimmer, Dick.
GV863.A1S25   1997   96-53557
796.357'0973--dc21   CIP

Reprint permissions are found on pages 207-210

Every reasonable effort has been made to obtain reprint permissions. If there has been an error, please notify the pub-
lisher. We will gladly correct any inadvertent errors or omis-
sions in subsequent editions.

Table of Contents

&

[III]

Contents

Contents

Contents

Acknowledgements
ॐ

Many thanks to Tom Bast and Holly Kondras of Masters Press for their continuing support and joyful spirits.

Credits:

Proofread by Pat Brady & Kim Heusel

Cover photo and design by Suzanne Lincoln

Introduction

ॐ

Oft times, in the wee small hours of the morning or in the smoggy pall of a freeway crawl, I'll replay once more the highlight reel of my one shining moment from a ball game long ago. Though I'm hardly alone in this, having frequently found friends from all walks of life who also harken back, eyes brightly glowing again as they spin out youthful athletic glories: a leaping, one-handed, over-the-fence catch at Matawan Regional High in the New Jersey State championships by a noted criminal attorney; a long foul homer at Yale, the best hit of his brief career by a second-string first baseman and now New York editor-in-chief; scoring from first on a looping single in a Westlake, California Little League final by a current Delta Airline pilot; or a booming twilight triple that cleared the bases at a New Hampshire summer camp by a gray-haired writer of Movies of the Week.

Introduction

And what follows are the literary equivalents of those timeless childhood moments, as well as the legendary exploits of our major league heroes: from Musial uncoiling to Mantle exploding, Marvelous Marv to Steve Dalkowsi, Jackie Robinson to Ken Griffey, Jr., Sandy Koufax to Roy "The Natural" Hobbs, splendid and unusual writings that explore the various aspects of the game we adore, all brilliantly caught like videos of prose.

The Sandlot Game

Thomas Boswell

ॐ

From Cracking the Show

Years from now, when ballplayers talk about the 1991 All-Star Game, their most vivid memory may be of what Cal Ripken did the day before the classic.

What Michael Jordan and Larry Bird have done for slam-dunk and three-point contests, Ripken did yesterday for the long ball. Forget the old "Home Run Derby" from 1950s TV. This was new legend.

In 22 swings, the Orioles shortstop hit an astonishing 12 home runs, including several that may have been longer than any he's hit in Memorial Stadium.

"Unbelievable," said Kirby Puckett. "Unbelievable," said Carlton Fisk. "Unbelievable," said Ripken himself.

No, not unbelievable.

However, to a game that can't afford to lose one more iota of its innocence, Ripken gave an indelibly sweet moment — one worthy of a man who hasn't missed a game in more than nine years.

"I didn't know what I was doing but I didn't want it to stop," said Ripken. "I felt like a little boy."

That's sure not how Ripken felt an hour earlier. Then, he was honestly worried. Was he going to risk wasting a year of work — as well as rediscovery of himself as a hitter — for the sake of this one gimmicky slugging contest?

"I hate these things. Nothing messes you up faster. Especially me. It puts me right back in all the bad habits I've worked so hard to break," he said. "When we go to Rochester (to play AAA farmhands), I won't be in them. When the guys have long ball contests before games in BP, I try to stay out of 'em."

"But I've agreed to be in this one. So I'll try to hit home runs. If I hit liners up the middle, it'd look bad."

A year ago at the All-Star break, Ripken was so humiliated by his .208 average that he dismantled his swing, stance, and strategy. Now, one July later, Ripken is leading the league in hitting (.348), total bases (190), and hits (111). He's hit 18 home runs and he's on pace for 36 for the season and 110 RBIs.

Finally, this year, the more he's looked out for No. 1, the better it's been for everybody. Of course, Ted Williams could have told him that.

"All right," said Ripken, finally, "I'm going to stick with what I've been doing all year. Everybody says you hit homers when you aren't trying. So let's see. Maybe I'll hit one by accident."

In last year's All-Star contest in Wrigley Field, the four-man AL team hit one homer. Yesterday, National Leaguers Howard Johnson and Chris Sabo each swung ten times without one. Other sluggers, such as Joe Carter of the Blue Jays and George Bell of the Cubs, hit a couple.

Ripken, however, was a bit different. After taking two

pitches from Toronto coach Hector Torres, he began his turn with a line drive to center. Except that the ball didn't want to come down until it smacked above a billboard 430 feet away.

After a liner to left, Ripken almost decapitated a vendor in the second deck in left center, about 440 feet away. Almost before that landed, his next blow reached the third deck, 450 feet away.

Ripken's next blow looked like a high liner over shortstop. But it kept working until it cleared the wall. An instant later, No. 5 hit the foul pole at third-deck level.

By now, the AL dugout was a madhouse of high fives, comic bows, and awestruck laughter. Oops, there it goes again — another 420-foot second-decker. On the eighth pitch, Ripken hit his seventh ball out of the park.

Finally, a warning-track fly and a popup gave Ripken his second and third outs. He headed to the dugout. Ten swings.

No way. The crowd wanted more. In what may have been an impromptu change of rules, the PA announcer sent Ripken back to the plate for a full ten outs.

First swing: another liner into the stands. Then after a rope through the box, two more 410-to-420-foot home runs. The crowd may not have known exactly how special this was, but every player did. "I've never done anything remotely like that," said Fisk, who has 360 career homers. "[In 22 seasons] I've only seen one player have a BP like that — Fred Lynn the year he hit 39 homers."

By this time — 10 homers in 14 swings — Ripken was worrying again. "I was getting arm-weary," he said. "I just wanted to make a couple of outs." Ripken even started shaking his arm as if he'd hurt his funny bone. "Maybe I did that subconsciously because I was embarrassed I was hitting so many."

After two line-outs and a popup, Ripken decided he'd try

to give the crowd a parting shot. "I decided," he said, "to dig down deep."

On the next swing, Ripken hit probably the longest ball of his life — a fourth-deck shot to left that came within a yard of joining Jose Canseco's 1989 playoff blast as the only fifth-deck homer in SkyDome lore. Distance? At least 475 feet. It was hard to tell. Because Ripken's next swing threatened to send the ball farther. But a brave fan in the third deck stopped it.

On his last two swings, Ripken merely knocked a ball off the left-field wall, then finished with a second-deck drive that hooked foul by a few feet.

Twelve home runs. On 22 swings.

"The Cal Ripken Hour," intoned the PA man. "What an exhibition!"

"Cal messed it up for everybody else," said Puckett. "Nobody wanted to go up and hit after that."

In all, seven other players in the contest took 85 swings and hit 15 home runs. The final score was NL 7, AL 8, Ripken 12.

For a long time afterward, Ripken could not get the grin off his face. Still, the face of the wary pro peered out from behind the dancing eyes of the little boy. It has cost Ripken years, and probably half of his hair, to get to .348. So, he worries.

"I kept trying not to overswing. But it was hard," he said when, once again, he was almost alone. "I hope this doesn't mess me up too bad."

1994

Jimmy Breslin

ह&

From Can't Anybody Here Play This Game?

Which brings us back to Marvelous Marvin Throneberry. On a hot Sunday last summer at old Busch Stadium in St. Louis. The Mets were in the field. Marvelous Marv was holding down first base. This is like saying Willie Sutton works at your bank.

It was the eighth inning of the first game of a double-header, and the Cardinals had Ken Boyer on first and Stanley Musial at third. Two were out. Boyer took a lead, then broke for second on the pitch. The throw to second from the Mets' catcher was, by some sort of miracle, perfect. It had Boyer beat by a mile, and the Cardinal runner, only halfway down, turned and tried to go back to first. The Mets' second baseman, Rod Kanehl, threw to Throneberry. Boyer was trapped.

Standard operating procedure in a situation of this kind is for the man with the ball to chase the runner, but with one eye firmly fixed on the man on third. If he breaks for home, you're supposed to go after him and forget the other guy.

So Boyer turned and started to run away from Throneberry. This seemed to incense Marv. Nobody runs away from Marvin Throneberry. He took after Boyer with purpose. He did not even wink at Musial. Marvelous Marv lowered his head a little and produced wonderful running action with his legs. This amazed the old manager, Casey Stengel, who was standing on the top step of the Mets' dugout. It also amazed Mr. Musial, who was relaxing on third. Stanley's mouth opened. Then he broke for the plate and ran across it and into the dugout with the run that cost the Mets the game. Out on the basepaths, Throneberry, despite all his intentions and heroic efforts, never did get Boyer. He finally had to flip to his shortstop, Charley Neal, who made the tag near second.

It was an incredible play. But a man does not become an institution on one play.

Therefore. There was a doubleheader against the Chicago Cubs at the Polo Grounds, the Mets' home until their new park is ready. In the first inning of the first game Don Landrum of Chicago was caught in a rundown between first and second. Rundowns are not Throneberry's strong point. In the middle of the posse of Mets chasing the runner, Throneberry found himself face to face with Landrum. The one trouble was that Marvin did not have the ball. Now during a rundown the cardinal rule is to get out of the way if you do not have the ball. If you stand around, the runner will deliberately bang into you and claim interference, and the umpire will call it for him, too.

Which is exactly what happened. Landrum jumped into Throneberry's arms, and the umpire waved him safely to first. So, instead of an out, the Cubs still had a runner at first — and the Mets were so upset, the Cubs jumped them for a four-run rally.

THE SANDLOT GAME

When the Mets came to bat, Throneberry strode to the plate, intent on making up for the whole thing. With two runners on, Marv drove a long shot to the bullpen in right-center field. It went between the outfielders and was a certain triple. As usual, Marv had that wonderful running action. He lowered his head and flew past first. Well past it. He didn't come within two steps of touching the bag. Then he raced to second, turned the corner grandly, and careened toward third. The stands roared for Marvin Throneberry. While all this violent action and excitement were going on, Ernie Banks, the Cubs' first baseman, casually strolled over to Umpire Dusty Bogges.

"Didn't touch the bag, you know, Dusty," Banks said. Bogges nodded. Banks then called for the ball. The relay came, and he stepped on first base. Across the infield Throneberry was standing on third. He was taking a deep breath and was proudly hitching up his belt, the roar of the crowd in his ears, when he saw the umpire calling him out at first.

"Things just sort of keep on happening to me," Marvin observed at one point during the season.

Which they did. All season long. And at the end, here was this balding twenty-eight-year-old from Collierville, Tennessee, standing at home plate with a big smile on his face as he proudly accepted a boat which he had won as the result of a clothing-store contest. Throneberry was not too certain what he would do with the boat. The most water he had seen in several years was a filled-up bathtub on Saturday night back in Collierville. The nearest lake to his house is 150 miles away, and 150 miles as the coon dog runs, Marv cautioned. "Take the road, it's a little further," he said.

ह्र

The whole season went this way for the Mets. Take any

[7]

day, any town, any inning. With the Mets nothing changed, only the pages on the calendar. It was all one wonderful mistake.

There was the Fourth of July, which certainly has significance, and the Mets were at Candlestick Park in San Francisco. Jim Davenport, the Giants' third baseman, swung at a pitch and lifted it high into the air. Rod Kanehl, the Met stationed at shortstop this time around, turned and raced into left field. Sunglasses flipping, glove up in the air, feet moving, Kanehl went for the ball.

The Mets' third baseman, Felix Mantilla, came in and made the catch right at the pitcher's mound.

ào

People simply loved the Mets. On June 17, when Marvelous Marvin Throneberry made his unforgettable maneuvers, messing up that rundown against the Cubs, then failing to touch first base, the fans were beside themselves when, right after Throneberry was called out, Charley Neal stepped in and hit a home run. Before Neal reached first, Casey Stengel stormed out of the dugout and held out his arm and pointed to first. Neal stepped on the bag. Then Stengel pointed to second. Neal stepped on the bag. Casey also pointed to third and to home plate and after Neal was across with the run, the old man nodded and went back to the dugout. The crowd roared.

1963

Peter Cohen

୬

From Diary of a Simple Man

For some reason (and if it were dis-
covered it would probably throw a good deal of light on the
dark side of my psyche) I have spent an unholy amount of
time either watching or thinking about baseball. When I was
eleven or twelve the Dodgers were always fighting it out with
the Cardinals, and I would lie awake at night working out
the pitching rotation for the next five games, and isn't it
lucky that Max Lanier jumped to the Mexican League and
why don't we get two million dollars together and buy Musial.
I hated Musial until it made me sick to think about him, but
when I went to Ebbetts Field and saw him at the plate I
forgot all about it because he was so wonderfully beautiful.
Standing there with his feet together, his shoulders hunched
and the bat almost straight up, he looked almost awkward,
and then Branca gave him the low outside fastball. Musial
took that sudden step, uncoiling like a spring, and then the
bat went around in a long sweep and there was the crack
that you never hear without wanting to stand up. Musial

was off digging for first, leaning into his stride, one fast look at Reese leaping straddle-legged for the ball, and then the ball was over the grass and then bouncing fast between Reiser and Hermanski, Hermanski lumbering slowly along the base of the wall and Reiser running at an angle to play the carom, taking it on the fly and throwing hard and low to Stanky at second, Musial going in with a casual slide, Jocko Conlan leaning down in the dust and then jabbing both arms out low at his sides. And there was Stan The Man Musial dusting himself off, standing on second base and saying something to Stanky. I couldn't hate him then.

As a matter of fact, when I *saw* the Cardinals I didn't hate any of them, excepting Harry The Cat Brecheen, but he was a pitcher. Next to Musial I loved Whitey Kurowski. One day in 1947 the Dodgers beat them in the rubber game of a three-game series late in August, and we knew Brooklyn would take the pennant if they could beat the Cardinals. Joe Hatten shut them out on six hits. Kurowski went 0-for-4 and made two errors and when he came out of the dressing room he was practically running. I guess he was going to Trommer's Beer Garden. I was one of a bunch of kids running along next to him trying to get him to sign our scorecards, and he was shaking his head and telling us to get out of here. Finally the other kids gave up and it was just me and Kurowski hurrying along Empire Boulevard in the sun. I was saying:

— Please Whitey lemme have you autograph

For the fiftieth time, when he stopped and put his bony Polish miner's face down to mine. There was a big ragged scar on his cheek and he glared at me and said:

— I SAID GET THE HELL OUT OF HERE

I ran all the way down the block before I stopped but even after that every time I saw him out at Ebbetts I loved him.

I like to go to a game by myself on a warm spring week-day afternoon. I get there early and sit back with my feet on the back of the empty chair in front of me. I get a couple of hot-dogs and a beer and watch them taking batting practice. Duke Snider is out in front of the left-field wall shagging flies, and from across the field you can hear the kids yelling:

— Hey Dook trow it up heah willya Dook comon trow it up heah.

The man behind me says to his friend:

— Why donee trow it to em?

— Waddya, crazy, if he trows em one deyll be on im alla time he wone get no rest.

— He ain suppose ta rest da crum he suppose ta be runnin aroun.

Snider turns towards the seats and lazily tosses up a ball and the kids are scrambling over the seats to get it.

— See, he trun it to em. He ain a bad guy.

— Yeah, dere's twona half bucks off his salry next year.

We all laugh. Campanella is batting with that funny round swing of his and he hits a couple well back into the upper deck.

— Ya see dat? He duzzat a couple times durina game we're in.

Batting practice is over and the field is empty, but the groundskeepers are out smoothing the infield dirt. The sun is comfortably warm and I order another beer and watch a large white cloud floating high over Bedford Avenue. After a while the batting orders start going up on the scoreboard and then Spahn and Erskine come out to warm up. The business goes on at home plate, the groundskeepers marking out the batter's boxes and the umpires taking the line-ups, and Erskine goes into the dugout but Spahn keeps throwing. He finally goes in and there's a quiet wait, and the Dodgers come out, fanning out to their positions while everybody yells, and then we all stand up to hear Gladys Gooding sing 'The Star-Spangled Banner.' I look around and see the stands are half-filled; the sun is warmer but not too hot, and there's a slight wind toward right field.

The Braves go down in the first, and when Reese walks to the plate the public address system says:

— Attention; now batting for Brooklyn; number one, Peewee Reese, shortstop.

And we all cheer extra loud because Team Captain Harold Peewee Reese is our lucky baby boy. While Spahn throws a last few warm-up pitches Reese stands watching him, still looking like a fresh-faced Boy Scout although he's been here for thirteen years. On the 2-2 pitch he flies deep to right and everybody starts calling:

— There it goes.

But I know it will be caught and I don't move. I am eighteen years old and I have been watching baseball games for a long time and I don't get excited about unimportant things.

There's no score up to the fourth when Robinson leads off with a single through the hole at shortstop. He is dancing off first base with Spahn watching him very calmly. Everybody is calling:

— Thataway Jackie baby.

And I am sitting on the edge of my seat saying:

— Go on you Jackie honey you.

The man behind me says:

— I hope he ain gunna try an steal on Spahnie. He duzzat he's outa his mine.

— Gan, he cud steal on any pitcha inna leeg.

Snider takes a ball and then pulls one foul, and on the next pitch Robinson is going, running pigeon-toed and barrel-chested, rocking on his hips. Crandall's throw is perfect but Robinson has it beaten, hooking his slide down and away. I am on my feet screaming:

— Way to go Jackie.

And everybody is roaring. Snider lines the next pitch into center field. Jethroe is charging the ball and in one corner of my eye I see Robinson rounding third. I stare at a point on the left-field line and open my eyes wide to see at the same time Jethroe scooping the ball and throwing and Robinson running for the plate. The throw is wide toward first base. Robinson crosses standing up while Crandall throws to second for Snider, but Dook is in safely and we are all going crazy. Campanella takes a strike and then the ball is high, high, unbelievably high over center field. I am on my feet with both fists in the air, holding my breath. Jethroe backs to the wall and then his arms drop at his sides and the ball bounces on the aisle in the center-field seats. Campanella trots around with his stomach jogging in front of him while Dook waits at the plate to shake his hand. The man behind me is pounding my back and yelling:

— I tolya I tolya he wuz gunna do it I tolya dint I?

— Yeah yuh tol me an I buhleved yuh dint I?

I turn around with a stupid grin on my face and say:

— Why aren't you guys here every day?

And we are friends for the rest of the afternoon. Two kids in the next section are calling:

— Guh wan Spahn, guh wan Spahn.

But he is standing with his hands on his hips looking at Hodges with the air of a man who has made a mistake in judgment that disgusts him slightly. He strikes out Hodges on five pitches and the crowd stops buzzing.

Nothing happens for the rest of the day until the Braves put two on in the ninth with two out and Adcock is up. Erskine still looks strong to me but I am worried and start on a small but tasteful prayer. One of my friends says:

— Adcock; whatzis foist name? Billy-joe ainit? No guy widda name like Billy-joe is gunna do nuttin.

I do not relax. Erskine puts one over at the knees, and then another low curve that Adcock beats down on the grass over the mound toward second base. I am standing again watching. Reese coming fast for the ball. He bends slightly and then the ball is going to Hodges who steps into the stretch like a man in a slow-motion movie: Dascolie with one hand on his knee jerks his thumb up for the out. I give a long sigh and listen to the crowd cheering. Campanella and Reese are patting Erskine's shoulders as they trot to the dugout.

Walking up Bedford Avenue the crowd is bumping into itself and laughing. I turn down Eastern Parkway. In the late afternoon sun the shadows of the trees are black on the gray stone and I can smell the peculiar fragrance of the city in the evening.

1961

Mark Gallagher, Paul Susman and Robert Schiewe

ع

From Explosion: The Legendary Home Runs of Mickey Mantle

Bovard Field, Los Angeles. He was more than a 19-year-old baseball player with a world of promise now. Mickey Mantle was something of a celebrity, and for good reason. He added shine to his star on this date by leading the New York Yankees' assault on the University of Southern California nine with a seven-RBI day, a day that included two legendary homers, a booming triple, and a leg single.

As Mantle tried to board the team bus afterward, he was mobbed by USC students, some seeking autographs, others reaching out to him, and all treating young Mickey as though he were a Hollywood film idol. The boy hadn't played one major-league game, but he was the most talked about ballplayer in the nation! As the Yankees concluded a golden California tour, Mickey was batting .432.

The Yankees may have beaten the collegians in a 15-1 rout, but these were the same Trojans who beat the Pittsburgh Pirates and the tough Pacific Coast League's Hollywood Stars. The same Trojans the Yankees went after, plucking 20 or so off the USC campus and giving big bonus money to several hot-shot kids who never made it. And here was Mickey, who was signed for next to nothing, exploding, of all places, on this very same campus.

Mantle hit eye-popping homers from each side of the plate. The left-handed homer was astonishing. Gil McDougald believes this was the longest ball he saw Mantle hit in their 10 seasons together with the Yankees. It was, he says, "certainly farther than the one he hit in Washington in 1953" (a 565-footer). Tommy Henrich says the ball "landed as far away from the fence as it was from the plate to the wall." USC coach Rod Dedeaux says it "was like a golf ball going into orbit. It was hit so far it was like it wasn't real."

Dedeaux, who has turned out major-leaguers by the bushel at USC, cites a football field that paralleled the outfield fence running from the right foul line to dead-center field; Mickey's ball left the baseball field near the 439-foot mark in right-center, Dedeaux says, sailed over the football field (160 feet wide with sidelines of some 40 feet each), and hit a fence on one hop.

According to Dedeaux, USC center fielder Tom Riach "virtually climbed the fence and hung on to the top, observing where the ball hit. Other people sitting in the stands confirmed the location." No doubt about it, says Dedeaux, "It was a superhuman feat."

Riach recalls shading the Mick to right and running to the right of the 439-foot sign as the ball headed his way. "I jumped up on the fence and watched the ball cross the football field and short-hop the fence to the north of the football field." On a scale drawing of the baseball and football fields, Riach puts the landing spot a shade longer than Dedeaux's point of impact, but the two landing spots are essentially side by side.

Researcher Paul Susman's friend and counselor in things mathematical, Robert H. Schiewe, on the basis of the Dedeaux and Riach accounts, calculates a travel distance of 645 feet from home plate to the Dedeaux dot and, incredibly, of 645 to 660 feet to the Riach dot.

The right-handed Mantle homer also witnessed by the record Bovard crowd of some 3,000 cannot be overlooked either. It soared over the fence in left at about the 351-foot mark, cleared a street and several houses, and landed on the top of a three-story house. This one had to exceed 500 feet.

1987

Bovard Field at the University of Southern California. The arrows show where Mantle's home runs went. He hit one from each side of the plate in an exhibition game on March 26, 1951. They say that the one that went across the football field went over 600 feet in the air. (Photo courtesy of Sagamore Publishers)

Willie Mays, as told to Charles Einstein

ະ♠

From Willie Mays: My Life in and out of Baseball

$\mathbf{A}$t the beginning, my daddy went to Piper Davis and said, "Give him a contract. He can play."

"He thinks he's DiMaggio," Davis said.

"What's wrong with that?"

"He's a smaller man, that's what wrong. More he copies himself after Joe D., more he's got to unlearn."

"Then unlearn him," my father said. "But he can play for you, and you know it."

"Ain't much money," Davis said.

"How much ain't much?"

"Seventy a month?"

"You're right. That ain't."

"I'll up it five every month he's over .300," Davis said.

"With you changing him around," my father said, "he'd never collect."

"Why don't you talk to him?" Davis said.

So my dad talked to me.

"I can get you down in the mill," he said. "Only trouble

is, once you get in you never get out. I think maybe you can make better money doing something else."

"Baseball?"

"Doesn't have to be baseball. You got a trade."

That "you got a trade" was a kind of a fancy way of saying I'd taken a special course in cleaning and pressing at school. The idea was, I could enter into that field for a living, and baseball could always be something extra on the side.

"I think I can play for Piper Davis," I said.

"So does he," my dad said. "He's got a lot he wants to teach you. Hit a curveball, quit crowding the plate, so forth and so on."

"Then what do you think?" I said.

"I think you like baseball," he said.

It was as simple as that.

No. Not quite that simple. Because the next night, for what was to be the last time, my dad and I played together on the same team. He was in center field. I was in left. He was something like 36, 37, at the time, but his condition was fine, and he could still go get them.

It was a game between a couple of factory teams, but they had some good ballplayers. And in the second inning, one of the hitters, a left-handed batter, looped a long, sinking liner to left-center, the wrong field for him, and I heard my father say, "All right, all right, let me take it!" But then I was aware that the ball was sinking and he was too far back, and I knew if I cut in front of him I could handle it, so I did, and caught it off the grass-tops.

And I knew also that I'd shown him up.

And he knew it.

I've never apologized to him for making the play.

He's never apologized to me for trying to call me off.

We both wanted the same thing — to get away from the

situation where I had to play side by side in the same out-field with my own father.

Because even the great Kitty-Kat was beginning to slow down, the same as his son will slow down, and the only thing worse than being shown up by youth is being shown up by your own flesh and blood.

Because then you got to pretend you like it.

I think he had four or five years, maybe more, of part-time ball left in his system, my old man, but he didn't play them. I went with the Barons, and "One in a family is enough!" he'd say happily to anybody who asked, but I'd gone and knocked him out of the one thing he loved and lived for, and he knew it and I knew it. It's great for a man to see his son do something he always wanted to do but couldn't. It's great for a man to see his son want to follow in his father's foot-steps.

But don't play in the same outfield together. It's like a father and a son chasing the same girl.

Things will never be the same between you again.

All I had to do was let him have that baseball for himself, out there in that twilight in left-center field.

I could have said: "Take it — it's yours!"

But I didn't. And I can't buy it back.

1966

Arthur Daley

ᨒ

From More Honors for Willie

Jimmy Dykes, the unfrocked manager of the Orioles, and Tom Sheehan, the chief troubleshooter for the Giants, were exchanging pleasant lies during the baseball meetings a week or so ago, when Willie Mays edged his way into the conversation. That was inevitable. No member of the Giant official family can talk for five full minutes without mentioning Willie the Wonder.

"Wait a minute, Tom," said Dykes, a needler without a peer. "You're not going to stand there and tell me that Willie Mays actually exists."

"Of course he exists," said Long Tom, starting to splutter in indignation. "Didn't you see the catch he made on Vic Wertz in the World Series?"

"I saw it," said Dykes firmly. "But I still don't believe it. That catch had to be an optical illusion. It was the greatest catch I ever saw in my life."

"A fair-to-middling catch — for Willie, I mean," said Sheehan with studied casualness. "I've seen him do better."

"What?" shrieked Dykes.

"I'm skipping over the play he made against the Dodgers in 1951," said Sheehan. "The one involving Carl Furillo and Billy Cox. Remember it?"

"Vaguely," said Dykes, completely shaken out of his pose of indifference. "I might as well ask you to repeat it because I suspect you intend to do it anyway."

"Now you're cooking with gas," said the appreciative Sheehan. "The score is tied with one out in the eighth and Cox is at third with the winning run. Furillo slams a line drive to right-center and Cox tags up. Willie races seven miles before spearing the ball with his glove, a marvelous catch. But he's facing the right-field wall and there's no way he can stop, wheel and make the throw home to head off the runner.

"At this time Willie is merely a 20-year-old kid who's been in the big leagues only a couple of months. He don't know nuthin' from nohow. So he figures out a new way to do it. He spins around, away from the plate in a reverse turn, and the ball is on the way to the plate before he's finished spinning. It goes on a line in the air for a perfect strike to Wes Westrum and Cox is dead, tagged out ten steps down the line."

"Whee!" whistled Dykes, properly impressed.

"But that wasn't his best catch," said Sheehan. "Here it is."

It isn't often that the urbane and slightly supercilious Dykes gets trapped into resembling an open-mouthed tube. But Long Tom had him trapped.

"This catch was so wonderful," said Sheehan, "that even the fellows in the press box didn't appreciate it because Willie made it look so easy. We were playing the Braves at the Polo Grounds and I was watching from Horace Stoneham's office above the clubhouse in deepest center field. It gave us an unusual vantage point.

"Bill Bruton was at bat and he's not a long-ball hitter. So Willie played him shallow. From where we sat it almost looked as though he was almost standing on second base. Well, sir, Bruton hit the longest ball he ever hit in his life. He hadn't even brought the bat around before Willie had started running. It was a screamer down that center-field alley.

"Willie kept racing toward us. He looked over his left shoulder. He glanced over his right shoulder. And all the time he's going full tilt as he turns his head, right or left, to follow the ball.

"He'll never make it," says Horace to me.

"Don't bet on it," I says to him.

"Willie looks to the left for the last time. He looks to the right. Then he reaches out his two hands in front of him with his back to the plate. And that ball sails smack over his head into his outstretched hands. One more step and Willie is on the cinders below us, which should show you how far he had to run. In my book, that was the greatest catch he ever made."

"Shut up," said Dykes weakly. "I've heard enough for one day."

1954

David Halberstam

ə.

From Summer of '49

In mid-June Joe DiMaggio got up one morning and stepped cautiously on the floor, expecting the pain to shoot through his foot once again. Miraculously, the pain was gone. He touched his heel with his hand. Until then it had felt hot to the touch. Now it felt normal. He began to smile. He walked around the apartment and felt no pain.

That day, for the first time in weeks, he went out for both lunch and dinner. On the street when people recognized him he was pleased. He was delighted to sign autographs. Soon, he decided to take batting practice. The team was on a western trip, but Gus Niarhos, a backup catcher who was injured, and Al Schacht, a former pitcher known as The Clown Prince of Baseball, were available. Schacht could still throw reasonably hard. For fielders they got a bunch of neighborhood kids who hung around the Stadium. The workout lasted an hour.

Soon DiMaggio expanded the workouts. He had Niarhos

hit fly balls to him, and he would run them down. He was easily winded, and his legs were not in shape, but there was no pain. The Yankees came home from their road trip, and he showed up at the park in uniform. No one asked questions about whether he was ready. One morning he called Curt Gowdy, who lived in the same hotel, and they drove out to the Stadium together so that Gowdy could watch him take batting practice. When he finished, Gowdy took a look at his hands. They were completely covered with bloody blisters caused by the batting.

"Jesus, Joe, look at that," Gowdy said.

"Oh, that's nothing, forget about that," DiMaggio answered. "I took too much batting practice, but that doesn't matter. There's no pain in my foot. That matters."

Cleveland was in town for the first series of the home stand and Lou Boudreau, the Cleveland manager, was also the manager of the American League in the All-Star Game. It was still two weeks away and Boudreau told DiMaggio he hoped he would be able to play. "I'm not even in the running," DiMaggio said, for the fans voted then.

"I think it could be arranged," Boudreau said.

After the first game with Cleveland, when everyone else had left the park, DiMaggio asked Niarhos to hit fly balls to him in the outfield for half an hour. Then he ran around the outfield a few times. Again there was no pain. After the Cleveland series, the Yankees had an exhibition game with the Giants at home before going up to Boston for three games. Stengel told DiMaggio simply to let him know when he was ready, and DiMaggio decided to try the exhibition game.

Before the game there was a home run-hitting contest, and by far the biggest cheers were for DiMaggio. He hit only one out, but it drew even wilder cheers from the crowd. He went hitless in four trips during the game, but the Giants had used Kirby Higbe, who was throwing a knuckle ball at the time. It was not the optimum pitch to return against. The next day the team left for Boston, and until the last minute DiMaggio did not know if he would make the trip. He was torn between the desire to play and the fear that he wasn't ready for real pitching. He did not want to embarrass himself and hurt the team. The other players went up by train in the morning. He waited and then finally jumped on a 3:15 plane. On the plane he saw a friend who asked if he was going to play. "I don't know," he answered. At 5:15 he arrived at the clubhouse. Stengel was surrounded by writers who were asking for the lineup. He was still waiting to hear from DiMaggio. DiMaggio was dressing slowly, pondering what to do, and Stengel was stalling the writers. Finally DiMaggio said yes, he could play, so Stengel put him in the lineup.

In their dugout the Red Sox watched DiMaggio come out to warm up. One of the younger Boston players predicted that DiMaggio would have a hard time running out an infield hit. McCarthy, a great DiMaggio fan, immediately interrupted him. "You don't know him. You watch him the first time there's a chance for an infield hit. Watch how he runs," he said. There was an ominous note to the way McCarthy said it, one of the Boston pitchers thought, as if he were saying, "*They* are the real professionals."

In the first game Mickey McDermott was pitching for the Red Sox. He was young, skinny, and wild. In the second inning DiMaggio led off. McDermott was very fast, one of the three or four fastest pitchers in the league. DiMaggio found it hard to adjust his batting eye to McDermott's speed and he fouled off six or seven pitches. Each one went off to the right, which meant that he was swinging late. Finally McDermott came in with a fastball, belt-high, and DiMaggio slapped it over Junior Stephens' head for a single. That was a hit well earned. Then Lindell walked and Hank Bauer hit a home run. The Yankees were up 3-0. In the third Rizzuto singled to start the inning, then DiMaggio came up again. That man, McDermott thought, does not seem to me like a player who has missed two months of play, that looks to me like the real Joe DiMaggio. On the mound he said a prayer: "Please, dear God, help me get this man out. I won't ask anything else from you today." Then, he remembers, "I heard this deep voice answering me: 'I'll help you get him out, Maurice, if you've got a really good fastball today. Other than that, son, you're on your own.'" He was, it appeared, on his own. This time DiMaggio put his body into a pitch and hit it over the wall. How sweet the feeling was. Rizzuto jumped up and down like a little kid as DiMaggio crossed home plate. The Yankees won 5-4 behind Reynolds and Page.

Ellis Kinder pitched the second game against Tommy Byrne. Byrne, a lefty, was intimidated by Fenway. He never made it past the first inning. He walked three and gave up three doubles in a row to Williams, Stephens, and Doerr. In the second, with the Yankees playing deep, Williams bunted for a hit and then Stephens hit a home run. The Red Sox took a 7-1 lead into the fifth. Even in Fenway, that was a huge lead against a tough pitcher. But in the fifth, Kinder seemed to lose his control. He walked Rizzuto and Henrich, which brought up DiMaggio. Kinder was a hard pitcher for DiMaggio, who preferred a fastball pitcher; Kinder usually relied on subtlety instead of power. This time, though, DiMaggio got the pitch he wanted and drove the ball over the fence in left-center. The score was now 7-4.

In the seventh Gene Woodling doubled off Earl Johnson with the bases loaded. In the eighth, with the score tied 7-7, and with two out and no one on, DiMaggio came up again against Johnson. The Boston fans, aware that something remarkable was going on, had started cheering for DiMaggio as well as for their own team. Johnson, the top Boston relief pitcher, was determined not to give DiMaggio anything good to hit. He was aware that Williams and DiMaggio were in a dead heat for the title of best hitter in baseball. A few years earlier, with a game on the line, Johnson had pitched to DiMaggio with two out and men on second and third. Joe Cronin had come out to the mound. "Whatever you do, Earl," he had said, "don't throw him a strike. Don't let him beat us." Johnson had placed the ball exactly where he wanted it, about six inches on the outside, but DiMaggio had pounced on it and, even more remarkably, pulled the ball past third for the game-winning hit. A few months later Johnson ran into DiMaggio at a postseason banquet. "Joe, how in the hell did you pull that ball?" Johnson asked. "I figured that when Cronin came out he told you not to give me anything good to hit. I was sure he told you to pitch on the outside. So I waited, and I was ready," he answered.

Johnson decided to give DiMaggio a low inside curve, a hard pitch for a hitter to get in the air. He put the ball exactly where he wanted it. To his amazement DiMaggio reached down and golfed the ball way over the wall and onto the screen. It was the hardest kind of swing for a good hitter, particularly one who was out of tune. As DiMaggio neared the dugout, Stengel, never one to miss an opportunity for theater, came out and starting bowing toward him like a Muslim to Mecca.

Even before the Boston game, DiMaggio's return had become, day-by-day, an occasion of national drama. Now it was a national sensation, so much so that he later sold his account of it to *Life* magazine for $6,000, a very large figure for the period. DiMaggio's own memory was of the noise and cheering, which grew and grew, inning by inning, until it was deafening.

That afternoon, in the locker room, DiMaggio teased Rizzuto, who had knocked in two runs. "What are you trying to do, steal my RBIs?" he asked. Rizzuto, who had played with him for almost a decade, had never seen him so playful. Spec Shea went over to him and asked if he was in any pain. "Nothing hurts when you play like this," he answered.

There was one game left. Raschi against Parnell — ace against ace that year: Raschi was 11-2 going in, Parnell was 10-3. If any Boston pitcher could stop DiMaggio in Fenway, it was Mel Parnell.

If there is such a thing as a natural in baseball, it was Parnell. He threw, both teammates and opponents thought, so effortlessly that it was almost unbelievable. He had fully intended to be a first baseman, not a pitcher. As a boy all he had wanted to do was hit. He played on a strong New Orleans high school team, where on occasion he would pitch batting practice to his teammates. "Stop throwing breaking stuff," they would yell, and he would explain that he was throwing fastballs.

One day a Red Sox scout was in town to scout a teammate. Parnell's team was short of pitchers, and his coach had asked him to pitch for the first time in his life. He struck out seventeen. The Boston scout, Ed Montague, reported back that they should go after Parnell. The Cardinals had already begun to make overtures to him and some of his high school teammates. In the thirties, the Cardinals under Branch Rickey had the best farm system in the country, and New Orleans was considered a Cardinal town. The local team, the New Orleans Pelicans, was a Cardinal farm team. Seven players from Parnell's high school team signed professional contracts, six of them with the Cards. A couple of times

Parnell pitched batting practice against the Pelicans and that heightened Cardinal interest. Soon Branch Rickey himself began to appear at the Parnell home. He was a dapper figure, very much the gent in derby hat and spats. Patrick Parnell, an engineer on the Illinois Central, loved to talk baseball, and here was one of the most famous men in baseball dropping in on him.

No one ever accused Branch Rickey of not being a wonderful salesman — whether he was selling God or major-league baseball or himself. He mesmerized the senior Parnell with stories of big-league baseball. Patrick Parnell thought Mr. Rickey a wonderful man and a religious man, but Mel Parnell took a harder look. Even though he was desperate to be a big-league ballplayer, he wanted no part of Branch Rickey or the Cardinals. They had a simple philosophy behind their system: Sign every talented kid they could for very little money, put them in a giant farm system, let them fight their way to the top, keep a handful of the best for themselves, and trade or sell a few others. (The penurious quality of the St. Louis organization was well known even within the largely penurious world of baseball. In 1948, the Cardinals had signed their great outfielder, Stan Musial, to a new contract of $28,000, the largest amount of money ever paid to a St. Louis ballplayer.) As their best players became slightly advanced, not so much in years as in salary, they would replace them with younger, less expensive players. In one period, between 1938 and 1942, the Cardinals sold off a number of their best players for a total of $625,000 while steadily improving their team. "How can I sell so many players and still come up with a winning team?" Rickey said in an interview. "I'll tell you. It's mass production! And by that I mean mass production primarily in tryout camps and mass production primarily of pitchers."

The Cardinals had three AAA teams, two AA teams and a host of lesser ones. The Cardinal Chain Gang it was called by players caught within it and unable to get out. Mel Parnell at seventeen was smart enough to know he wanted something different. He had heard about Rickey's sales pitch — golden tongued, yet homey, and was wary of succumbing to it. Therefore, on the frequent occasions that Branch Rickey showed up at the Parnell house, Mel Parnell did not come home until he was sure that their guest had gone.

He signed with Boston, and entered the Boston farm system at the age of twenty. Parnell moved up quickly, and might have made the majors by the time he was twenty-five except for World War II, which took three years out of his career. By 1948 he was ready to pitch in Fenway. That part did not come naturally. He had been purely a power pitcher until then. But power pitchers, he knew, particularly left-handed ones, died young in Fenway. Howie Pollet, a talented young Cardinal pitcher who was a friend in New Orleans and who had pitched in Fenway in 1946, warned Parnell, "Mel, you can't do it with the fastball. You'll go up in big games against the best hitters in baseball and they'll just sit on it and kill you." So Parnell developed a slider by holding the ball differently, off the seams. Also, Joe Dobson, who had the best curve on the team, taught him something about throwing the curve. It was not a lesson that began well. "Dobson," Parnell told Dobson, "why don't you get the hell out of here — I know more about pitching than you'll ever know." Parnell and his friend Mickey Harris, who was also young and talented and left-handed, specialized in being cocky and fresh. They drove Joe Cronin crazy. "The two wise asses," he would call them. Cronin would see them near the bench and he would say, "Out of here, you two wise asses, get out. Get down to the bullpen. Anywhere, but get out of here."

Parnell was determined to figure out Fenway. Most pitchers, particularly left-handers, fearing the Wall pitched defensively — outside to the right-handers. Parnell refused to buckle under. He would pitch inside and tight, especially to such big, powerful hitters as Lindell, DiMaggio, Keller, and Billy Johnson. He would pin their arms in against them so that they could not gain true leverage. It was later said that Hank Bauer and Mickey Mantle broke so many of their bats against him on sliders coming in to the narrow part of the bat that they felt he should buy them new ones. The hard part of pitching in Fenway, Parnell believed, was not the Wall. Rather it was the lack of foul territory. The stands were right on top of the field. It was a fan's delight but a pitcher's nightmare, because a good many foul balls that were caught in other parks went into the stands at Fenway. A nine-inning game at Fenway would have been a ten-inning game anywhere else.

Statistics are not always the best gauge of players, but in Parnell's case they are unusually revealing. In 1949 his earned-run average at home was 2.59, and on the road it was 3.02; for his career, his Fenway earned-run average was just slightly under his road one.

જાત

The Yankees were leading 3-2 in the seventh, a narrow margin in Fenway on a day when Raschi was in the process of giving up 12 hits. Again it came down to DiMaggio against the Red Sox pitcher. Stirnweiss had singled. Rizzuto had made the second out of the inning. Then Henrich had singled. Parnell stepped off the mound to think for a minute. He essentially called his own pitches. He did not trust catchers to do it because he did not think they had a feel for pitching; they could not, for example, *feel* the ball and know that the stitches on each ball are different, and as the stitches are different, the pitcher's finger control is different. Parnell liked to take each ball, feel the stitches, and then make his own decision.

On this day his best pitch was his fastball, and he decided to go with it. The one thing he was not going to throw Joe DiMaggio was a change-up. As a rookie he had been in the bullpen during a series in the Stadium, and DiMaggio had come to the plate. Bill Zuber, a veteran pitcher, called Parnell over. "Kid," he said, "whatever you do, don't throw this guy a change. If you do, he'll hit it into the third deck." A few innings later, the Red Sox were in trouble. Zuber went into the game with DiMaggio up and men on base. To Parnell's amazement, Zuber threw a change. DiMaggio hit it into the third tier. It hooked foul at the last moment. Zuber pitched again. Another change. Again DiMaggio jumped on it, and this time it carried into the third tier, fair. That was the game. Afterward, Parnell saw Zuber in the locker room hitting his head against the wall, saying, "Dumb Dutchman! Dumb goddamn Dutchman! I tell the kid not to throw the change and then I do it myself! Dumb goddamn Dutchman."

DiMaggio was a great hitter on a tear, and if Parnell was going to win, he wanted to win with his best pitch, and if he was going to be beaten, it might as well also be with his best pitch. His first pitch was a fastball just where he wanted it; DiMaggio lifted a high foul to the right side of the infield. Parnell breathed a sigh of relief. Billy Goodman was playing first, and the ball hit the heel of his glove and dropped out. Strike one. Parnell came back with the same pitch. Again DiMaggio fouled it off, this time with a squiggly little ball near the plate. Parnell began to feel very confident because he had DiMaggio 0-and-2. This time he decided to make him go fishing, and threw just off the outside corner. Another batter behind in the count might have gone for it. DiMaggio did not. Ball one. Parnell decided to waste another one, this time on the inside. Again DiMaggio did not bite. Parnell did not want to come in to DiMaggio on a 3-and-2 count and so he threw his best fastball. With a great hitter like DiMaggio, finally you challenged him. DiMaggio, who had been waiting for a fastball, killed it. The ball hit the steel towers in left field. For the next five minutes Parnell was sure that all Joe DiMaggio could hear was the cheers of the crowd, while the only thing he could hear was the steel ringing from the impact of the ball. Over Fenway flew a small biplane trailing a banner that said: THE GREAT DiMaggio.

It made the score 6-2. Raschi finished the game, and the Yankees swept the series. DiMaggio, in three games, had absolutely demolished the Red Sox: four home runs and nine runs batted in. It was the sweetest of all returns, and after that game, in the madness of the Yankee locker room, DiMaggio walked past Jerry Coleman and grinned, which was unusual; it was as close as he ever came to boasting or gloating. "You can't beat this life, kid," he said.

1989

W.C. *Heinz*

ﾞ❧

The Fireman
From Once They Heard the Cheers

*The Yankees beat the Dodgers in the Series because
I had an edge on Burt. I had DiMaggio and Page.
Gentlemen, I give you Joe DiMaggio...and Joe Page.*
— **Bucky Harris**

We drove east out of Texas and across seven states and into western Pennsylvania. It took us three days, and I called him on the phone from South Hapeville, Georgia, and then from Beckley, West Virginia, to let him know where we were and when we might be in.

"How are you tonight?" I said the last night out, and when he answered his voice was flat and tired-sounding again.

"Oh, so-so, Billy," he said. It was what he had said two nights before.

"Only so-so?" I said.

"Yeah, Billy," he said. "When you coming in?"

"I figure we should be there early tomorrow afternoon," I said. "Will you be there then?"

"I'm here all the time," he said, the voice the same.

The address the Yankees had given me was in care of Joe Page's Rocky Lodge, Route 30, Laughlintown, Pennsylvania. Both times that I had called he had answered the phone himself and almost immediately, and so I had pictured him perhaps in a small office or maybe picking up a phone at the end of a bar.

"We'll need a couple of rooms for a night," I said. "What is Joe Page's Rocky Lodge?"

"It's a small inn," he said, "but I don't have any rooms. You won't have any trouble getting rooms in Ligonier, though, and that's only three miles. There's a couple of good motels there."

"Don't worry about it," I said. "I'll be there tomorrow."

"Sure, Billy," he said.

"He's not well," I said to Skipper Lofting after I had hung up. "He's real down, the same as the other night. I'm sure he's in poor health, and that makes me feel like a louse. I should know."

"How would you know?" Skipper said. "How many years is it?"

"It was 1950," I said, "and I said good-bye to him in the Yankee clubhouse at the Stadium. The White Sox had just knocked him out of the box. I think it was Aaron Robinson who doubled in the winning run, and he used to catch Joe in the minors and on the Yankees before they traded him to Chicago. Two days later they sent Joe down to Kansas City, which was a Yankee farm club then."

"That was twenty-six years ago," Skipper said.

"That's what's wrong with this business," I said. "We're a lot of hustlers. We latch on to someone because he's in the public eye and we need to make a living. We plumb his background and pick his brain. We search out his motivations and his aspirations, and if he's a good guy, an association, even a friendship, forms. Then we say good-bye and good luck, and if his luck runs out where are we? We're long gone, and on to somebody else."

"You can't be everybody's brother," Skipper said, "and besides, I'm getting hungry. When are you figuring to eat?"

When he had it, in '47 and '49, he was one of the great relief pitchers of all time. He was a fastball left-hander who, as the expression used to go, threw aspirins. Baseball, in New York at least, was reaching its peak of post-war popularity, and for the crucial games, and for those two World Series, of course, the Stadium would be packed. I can still see it the way it was in the late innings, the Yankee pitcher faltering with men on the bases, the conference on the mound, then Bucky Harris in '47 and Casey Stengel in '49 taking the ball from the pitcher and signaling with his left hand. In the stands 70,000 heads would turn and 70,000 pairs of eyes would fasten on the bullpen beyond right field.

"Now coming in to pitch for the Yankees," the voice of the public address announcer would sound, echoing, "Joe Page!"

It was like thunder, rolling, and it made a cave of the vast Stadium. They rose as one, all their shouts and screams one great roar, and the gate of the low chain-link fence would open, and he would come out, immaculate in those pinstripes, walking with that sort of slow, shuffling gait, his warm-up jacket over his shoulder, a man on his way to work. In '47 he was in fifty-eight games, of which the Yankees won thirty-seven, including the seventh against the Dodgers in the Series. In '49 he appeared in sixty, forty-two of which the Yankees won, and in the Series he saved two, again against Brooklyn.

He was six feet three, perfectly proportioned at 215 pounds, and he was handsome. He had a smooth oval face, dark hair, blue eyes and a smile that, in those days, could have sold Ipana toothpaste. Of all the Yankees only Joe DiMaggio, his buddy and roommate on the road, surpassed him in popularity. After the '47 Series, a Mr. and Mrs. Bernard MacDougall, in Inverness, Nova Scotia, named their son Joe Page MacDougall after him.

He was the oldest of seven children, and his father had been a miner in the coal fields along the Allegheny just northeast of Pittsburgh, and he himself had worked in the mines for two years. As a rookie with the Yankees in 1944, he made the All-Stars, but the night of the game his father died. A sister had been killed in an automobile accident earlier that year, and his mother had passed away the year before. He was married then to Katie Carrigan, whom he had known since they were children, and now he became the main support of three sisters and two brothers, the oldest eighteen and the youngest eleven.

"I had written a piece for *Cosmopolitan* called 'Fighter's Wife'," I was telling Skipper Lofting, "about Rocky Graziano's wife, Norma. The night he fought Charley Fusari, when it started to come over the radio she ran out of the house, and I walked the streets with her and then waited with her until he came home. Then I got an assignment from *Life* to do 'Ballplayer's Wife' with Katie and Joe. When the Yankees would come off the road for a home stand, I'd sit with her in the wives' section, waiting for Joe to come in and save the game.

"I sat there with her for four weeks in all, and it was sad. In would come Joe, and he just didn't have it any more. When a speed-ball pitcher loses just that little bit off it, those hitters who have been standing there with their bats on their shoulders just love it. They tee off, and it is brutal. Sometimes we'd go to dinner afterwards, and I'd try to console them, but it wasn't any good.

"That last game he pitched for the Yankees, after he lost it, I left Katie and went down to the clubhouse to tell him she'd be waiting in their car. He always had the dressing stall next to DiMaggio, and he was sitting there with his head down. I said 'Joe, tough luck.' He looked up at me, and he said, 'Billy, you're jinxin' me.'"

"Well," Skipper said, "you know how superstitious ballplayers are, or used to be."

"I know," I said, "but he meant it right then. He was grasping for anything. I said, 'You might be right, Joe, and I'm dropping the story.' I told him he'd probably get it back his next time out, and I wished him luck and shook hands, and I left. End of story."

"I guess you couldn't write about losing in those days," Skipper said.

"Only in literature," I said.

Now, after we had checked in the motel in Ligonier and had lunch, we drove southeast out of town on Route 30, the mid-December sun lowering behind us, and then through Laughlintown. Where the road started to rise toward a ridge, stands of hardwood crowded it on both sides, and then on the right we saw the blue sign with the white letters: Joe Page's Rocky Lodge. Set among the trees was a three-story building of fieldstone and wood, and the only vehicle in the parking space in front was a light blue pickup.

I got out of the car, and on the gravel of the shaded drive-way there were patches of frost and on some of the dry, brown leaves a light sugaring of dry powder snow. Drapes had been drawn across the first floor windows of the building, and as I reached the door under the overhang, I heard the lock turn. I could hear the sounds of a football game on a television, and I knocked on the door.

"We're closed," a voice said.

"I'm Bill Heinz," I said. "Joe Page is expecting me."

"Oh," the voice said, and then the lock turned again and the door opened, and he said, "I'm his son Joe."

"And you look like him," I said, as we shook hands. He was in his late teens and wearing glasses with narrow steel rims, but it was there in the blue eyes.

"That's what people say," he said, smiling.

"I have a friend with me," I said. "I just want to go back to the car and bring him in."

He waited at the door, and I introduced Skipper to him. The barroom, deserted, was to the right, and he led us to the left into a long, darkened room, the only illumination coming from ceiling lights in the back. To the left, against the front wall, there was a juke box, and next to it the television. On the right a log fire was going in a fieldstone fireplace, dining room chairs and small tables were stacked against the other wall, and in an armchair his father was sitting. He got up slowly and walked toward me.

"You look good, Billy," he said putting out his hand. "A little heavier."

It was Joe Page, all right, but I knew it only by those eyes. That dark hair was gray now, and his mouth was shrunken. The left side of his jaw was hollow behind a gray beard of several days, his neck was thin, and that great left arm hung loosely at his side.

"How are you, Joe?" I said.

"Oh, so-so," he said.

I introduced Skipper to him, and he introduced his younger son Jon, who was seventeen, and two years younger than his brother, and Bryan Miller, a young friend of Jon's who had come in to watch on TV the Washington Redskins and Minnesota Vikings in their National Football Conference playoff game. We found straight-back chairs, and he sat down slowly again in the armchair, as I tried to find a way to ask the question.

"Cancer of the throat," he said, while I was still groping. "It tears the hell out of you, the muscles all the way down. I can't shave. They took all my teeth, and just left me two, and I can't eat."

"When was that?" I said.

"In 1973," he said. "In August of 1970, I had the heart attack at the Old Timers Game. I walked up in the stands and started to sweat and couldn't talk. They sent me down to Lenox Hill Hospital, and then I come home and had the open heart at St. Francis in Pittsburgh."

"They've really been beating up on you," I said.

"That's what happened to my arm," he said, reaching across with his right and rubbing his left arm. "These fingers go numb. They want to give me a new jaw, but I don't know if I'll get it. They cut me enough, and I've got a hernia now, too."

I was groping again, but on the TV the announcer's voice and the crowd noise had risen, and his eyes went toward the set. In the backfield Fran Tarkenton was scrambling, with two big Redskin linemen lumbering after him, and then he released the ball and it fell short of a receiver who was coming back for it.

"How long have you had this place?" I said.

"Seventeen years ago I bought it," he said. "First I had one down in Irwin called 'The Bull Pen.' I closed up here about three months ago. I couldn't take that stuff at the bar any more. You ever see any of the guys?"

"No," I said. "I've been writing other things."

"I miss all you guys," he said. "It was a strange life, but once you're out of it there was nothing else like it. DiMag was here, though. They give me a testimonial, and he come in from Frisco. The same old Daig. When was that, Joe?"

"It was two years ago," young Joe said.

"They had Spec Shea and Tommy Henrich," he said. "It was a nice party. Seven hundred people. The Daig was the same old Daig. He asked me about my back."

"I heard he had trouble with his back," Skipper Lofting said.

"That's right, Skip," he said. "I told him I had jammed up vertebrae and they opened it and straightened it out, and that's been fine ever since. You see him on that TV commercial? What's that thing he's doin'?"

"For the coffee maker?"

"Yeah," he said. "He sent me one. I got the filter, but not the maker."

"When I watch him on those commercials," I said, "I remember a story Frank Graham told. It was a couple of years after Joe came up to the Yankees, and he was still very shy and very quiet. They were at Shor's — Frank and Toots and Joe and a couple of others at a table — and Lefty Gomez stopped by. He told some story, as he can, and made a couple of quips, and when he left, Joe said, 'Gee, I wish I could be like that.'"

"He's some Daig," he said. "When Joe wasn't hittin', you remember that Del Prado where we stayed in Chicago? They had those big mirrors on the doors, and at five o'clock in the morning I'd hear him, and he'd be up there in front of the mirror practicing hittin'."

"One year," I said, "the Giants and the Dodgers opened the season in Brooklyn the same day that you people opened at the Stadium. Joe had the bad heel then, and he wasn't playing, and the next day, when Jimmy Cannon and I walked into the clubhouse, he was taking a treatment. He asked us where we'd been the day before, and we told him we'd been to Ebbets Field. He said, 'Where was the wind?' Jimmy said, 'Behind the hitters.' Joe said, 'The same here. I was coming up here in the taxi and there's a flag on a building about four blocks away and I always look at that to see where the wind is. The wind was just right. It broke my heart.' He was probably the only guy on the ballclub to check the wind before he got there, and he did it even when he wasn't playing."

"He's some Daig," Page said, "and Yogi's still goin' all right."

"He was another shy one," I said.

"Yeah," he said. "You're right." When Yogi Berra came up to the Yankees to stay in 1947, they almost hazed him out of the league, the other Yankees among them. They mocked his squat, early primate appearance and quoted his malaprops, until Bucky Harris, who was managing them then, put a stop to it. In the seventeen years that Yogi caught for the Yankees, he played in fifteen All-Star games and three times won the American League's Most Valuable Player Award, and in 1972 they elected him to the Hall of Fame.

"It was touch-and-go with Yogi for a while," I said now, "before Bucky straightened you guys out on him."

"Yeah," Page said. "We had a meeting and he told us to lay off. He told a few of the writers, too."

"I remember the day before the '47 series opened," I said. "You people had worked out at the Stadium and several of us writers were hanging around the clubhouse. They had the table in the middle of the room, with the cartons of balls to be autographed, and Yogi and Spec Shea were sitting there and signing. One of us asked Shea how he felt as a rookie about to pitch, the next day, the opening game of the World Series, and he said something about it being just another ballgame where you still just had to get twenty-seven outs."

"Yeah," Page said. "He would have said that. He was like that."

"So Yogi said, 'Yeah, but them shadows come awful early here this time of year.' He was worrying about those hits, with the ball coming out of the sunlight and then into the shadow of those three decks."

"That's the way it is there."

"Then one of the writers said, 'Come on, Yogi, stop worrying about it. You don't figure to get a hit, anyway.' With that, he and the others walked away. Yogi was sitting there with a ball in one hand, a pen in the other, and he said in that low voice, kind of to himself, 'Them writers think I'm kiddin', but they don't have to get up there and hit. They don't have to do nothin'.'"

"Yogi said that?"

"Yes," I said, "and it's a truth I have never forgotten, any time I have interviewed an athlete, or any time I have had to lay a critique on one."

"Yogi was the best receiver I ever pitched to," he said.

"And he could snap that bat," I said. "He had great wrists, so he could wait on the pitch. That's why he could get around on the breaking stuff, and even reach those bad balls."

"And he had a brain," he said.

"Which a lot of people found hard to believe at first," I said. "I remember that night game at the Stadium against the Red Sox — the game that made you. The bases were loaded, and you threw three balls to Rudy York, and Yogi came out from behind the plate and waddled up to you. As you two stood talking, somebody in the press box next to me said, 'This is ridiculous. What can he tell him?'"

It was May 26, 1947, and there were 74,000 in the stands that night, and all that Joe Page became and all that hap-

pened to him afterward stemmed from it. The Washington
Senators had knocked him out in the first start that season,
and several times he had failed in relief. In the third inning,
with the Red Sox leading, 3-1, two men on base and nobody
out, Bucky Harris brought him in for a last try. He got Ted
Williams to ground to George McQuinn, a great glove man,
but McQuinn bobbled it. Now the bases were loaded, and he
threw those three balls to York and, as Yogi walked to the
mound, Bucky Harris had one foot up on the dugout steps,
and Joe Page was one pitch away from the minors.

"I forget what Yogi said," he said now.

York took two strikes, and then he swung at the fastball
and missed. The count went to 3 and 0 on Bobby Doerr, and
again Harris was at the steps and again the future of Joe
Page hung on the next pitch. He threw strikes past Doerr,
and got Eddie Pellagrini to lift an easy fly ball up into that
rising thunder of sound for the third out. The Yankees won,
9-3, and Joe Page was on his way.

"Yogi knew baseball," he said now.

"I know," I said. "You guys won the opening game of that
'47 Series, but Yogi had a terrible day. He went 0-for-4, and
Burt Shotten had Peewee Reese and Jackie Robinson running. They each stole second, with Yogi bouncing the ball
down there, and afterward he was sitting in his dressing
stall, with his head down. I said to him, 'Yogi, forget it. You
guys won, and you'll have a better day tomorrow.' He said, 'I
guess I ain't very smart.' I said, 'Yogi, let me tell you something. I once asked you about last year when the Cardinals
were in the Series and you were home in St. Louis. I asked
you if you went to the games, and you said, 'No, I don't like
to watch games.' I said, 'Why not?' You said, 'It makes me
nervous, just to watch.' It makes you nervous to watch because you're always playing the game. Don't even think that

you're not smart enough, because you have a fine baseball brain. And Yogi said, 'I don't know. I don't know if you're right.'"

"Bucky knew it," he said now. "Bucky was the best manager I ever played for, but I was sorry when Stengel died. Rough to work for, you know? I'd come in, and Casey would come out talkin', but I never knew what the hell he was saying."

"You weren't the only one," I said.

"After I had the operations," he said, "I saw Yogi in New York at the Old Timers Game, and he didn't recognize me with this hollow neck. Jon said to him, 'It's my dad, Joe Page.'"

Young Joe had left the room. As he returned I watched him walk across in front of the television and its screen filled with a close-up of uniformed bodies and the sound voluming, and then sit down.

"He walks like you," I said. "When I watch him walk, I can see you coming in from that bull pen."

"The pup's got it, too," he said, nodding toward Jon. "I hope you get a chance to meet the wife. Mildred, but we call her Mitz. In 1954 I got married with Mitz. I think it was 1954. She's great. She's got her own insurance business, and I think she'll be back soon."

She came in a few minutes later. She is slim and dark-haired, and he introduced us to her. She took off her coat and she was wearing a denim jump suit. Skipper pulled up another straight-back chair, and she sat down between him and Joe.

"What have you been talking about?" she said.

"The old days," Joe said.

"I can imagine," she said.

"Do you ever get people dropping in here," I said, "who

see the sign outside and wonder if it's the real Joe Page?"

"Oh, yeah," he said. "Quite a few people. A guy would come in and say, 'Are you...?' and I'd say, 'Yeah.'"

"One guy came in," young Joe said, "and he said, 'I'm from New York, and I'd like to take Joe Page to dinner.'"

"Joe was in the hospital then," Mitz said. "I told the boys, 'If anybody comes in, don't tell them your dad's in the hospital.' So he told him, 'He's not in now, but if you want to see my mother, she's at work.' He came to the office, but I was at a restaurant, and when I came back to the office he'd gone.

"He came back here," she said, "and our other son here told him, 'My dad's in the hospital, and you can't see him.' I'd gone to the hospital by then, and this fellow came in. I told him he couldn't see Joe, and he said, 'I have to. When your husband was pitching, I was five years old. I sold newspapers, and one night I fell asleep where I was selling them. Your husband came along and he saw me there, and he woke me up and he said, 'You have to go home and sleep.' I said, 'I can't, until I sell these papers.' Your husband bought all my papers, and then he took me in and fed me. That's why I have to see him.'

"By now," she said, "he had the nurses and the doctor and me in tears. So we took him in to see Joe, and when we came out he told me, 'If there's anything you need, money or anything, just let me know.' He's a fine man."

"He must be," I said.

"He does hair replacement," she said, and then to young Joe, "Find that card he gave me."

On the business card was imprinted, "International Transitions Center." Under that, "Orange, Conn." Then, in the lower right corner, "George De Rosa, President."

"Where was it," I said to Page, "that you found him asleep and took him in to eat?"

"Patsy's," he said. "You remember we used to eat there? At 112th Street?"

"I remember," I said.

We went there a couple of times, after those bad ballgames, when I was trying to console them. I would be trying to get their minds off the game, and so I would get him to talking about what it had been like growing up playing ball around Springdale. The field had been cleared of rocks and stumps, but it was uphill to first and second base, and downhill from third to home. They traveled in the Lockerman's Meat Market panel truck, but they had no money for tires, so they packed them with sod and wired them to the rims.

"I don't suppose," I said now, "that Lockerman is still in business with his meat market."

"Yeah," he said, "the sons are."

"Sam and Jim and Howard," young Joe said.

"They come up to see Joe once in a while," Mitz said.

"I was telling Skipper," I said now, "about the last time I saw you in '50, in the clubhouse right after last time you pitched for the Yankees. I was working on that magazine piece that never came off, and you looked at me and you said, 'Billy, you're jinxin' me.'"

"I didn't mean it," he said now.

"I understood," I said. "You were reaching for anything. As I remember it, it was Aaron Robinson who'd got a double off you."

"I don't think so," he said. "Them left-hand hitters didn't hit me. After this throat, though, I couldn't remember nothin'."

"His memory was bad for a while," Mitz said.

"My back's givin' me hell now, too," he said.

"They took his lymph glands," she said.

She got up. She pushed her chair back and, standing behind his, began to knead his shoulder muscles.

"That feels good," he said.

"I think it was Aaron Robinson, though," I said, "because I was struck by the irony of it. He'd caught you on the way up, in Augusta and Newark and then on the Yankees, and it was his hit that sent you down to the minors."

"He was a hell of a catcher," he said. "He took a bottle of Seagram's to bed with him every night."

"He's dead," Mitz said.

"Yeah," he said, turning his head and touching the left side of his neck again. "Cancer."

"I'm sorry to hear that."

"You read what that Lopat said about me?" he said. Eddie Lopat was a left-hander who threw breaking stuff for the Yankees from 1948 to 1955.

"No," I said.

"That Lopat blasted me," he said. "It was in that book they wrote about Joe. They talked to people about Joe, and that Lopat was never in my apartment and he said I used to drink all night and come out the next day. He said I was lushed up every night, so how could I be ready sixty times a year?"

"I don't know," I said. "I didn't read the book."

There was that time, though, in '46, I was thinking, when Joe McCarthy let you have it out on the team plane two days before he quit managing the club. He figured you couldn't find the plate during the day because you'd touched too many bases the night before.

"Then a couple of days after I left you that last time," I said, "they sent you down to Kansas City."

"Casey never called me in the clubhouse," he said. "He saw me in the dugout, and he said, 'I've got your pink slip.' I said, 'Where am I goin'?' He said, 'Kansas City.'"

"What was that like?"

"Bad," he said. "That was more like a rest home. Johnny Mize was there with something wrong with him. Then I went to Frisco under Lefty O'Doul. That was bad, too. Cold, nobody in the stands and all that goddamn dampness. I never worked for a ballclub like I did here."

He came back up to pitch in seven games for Pittsburgh in 1954. His record that year was 0 and 0, and that was the end of it.

"The Old Man," he said, meaning Branch Rickey, who was trying to rebuild the Pirates then with youth, "had kids. They had kids from all around, and we called them 'Rickey dinks.'"

While we had been talking, the game on television had finished, the Vikings winning on their way to the Super Bowl. Jon stood up and said he would be going out for a while, and he and his friend shook hands with Skipper and me and left.

"The buck's a good football player," Joe said. "They call him 'The Monster.'"

"He's got a lot of schools looking at him," young Joe said.

"What does he play?"

"Linebacker and fullback," Page said, and he got up out of the chair. He walked slowly to the front door and opened it and went out.

"Where's he going?" Mitz said.

"To get wood," young Joe said.

"You should get it," she said.

When he came back in he was carrying two splits of log. He bent over and put them on the fire.

"They didn't call him 'The Fireman' for nothing," she said, as he sat down. "You watched him pitch. He was always arrogant, and that's the way our youngest son is."

But that was just the pose I was thinking. When he used to walk in there, he told me once, with those men on base and the thousands screaming, he could feel his heart pumping, and he said it seemed as if his stomach and all its contents were coming up into his throat.

"There was a fellow here from Bethany College, who was watching Jon," she said. "He said, 'You know, I don't think you'll ever make it in football.' Jon said to me, 'You know, Mom, I told him, 'I don't know about football, but I'm gonna make it somewhere.' He's just like his father."

As he walked from that bullpen, Tommy Henrich, in right field, would say to him, "Joe, you stop them, and we'll win it for you." Frank Crosetti, who was coaching then, told him, "If you knew how scared they are of that fastball, Joe, you wouldn't worry about anything." When his control would begin to go and he would start to miss the plate, "Snuffy" Stirnweiss would come trotting over to the mound from second, and he'd say, "You're not bearing down on the left leg again, Joe." It would get him out of it.

"That was sad about Stirnweiss," I said now.

"Snuff?" he said. "Yeah, I read about it. Sad."

One morning in September 1958, three cars of a commuter train out of New Jersey plunged through an open liftbridge into Newark Bay, and Stirnweiss was one of the more than two dozen who drowned in the cars. He had been a fine baseball and football player at the University of North Carolina, and he played for the Yankees from 1942 until 1950, once winning the American League batting championship, once setting a major-league fielding record for second basemen, and twice, with his speed, leading the league in stolen bases.

"What struck me when I read about it," I said, "was that

the speed that made him such a great athlete cost him his life. Someone, who had seen him get on the train, said that when he arrived at the station it was pulling out and he ran to catch it."

"You remember," he said, "how the first thing he'd do when he'd get on the train was go to sleep? I thought of that."

"In the last game of the '47 Series," I said, "when you threw that spitter to Gil Hodges, did he pop it up to Stirnweiss?"

"No, I struck him out," he said, "but it wasn't a spitter. That was the oil, the graphite oil. I used to keep it inside my belt."

"You told me it was a spitter," I said. "In the clubhouse, during the celebration, I came over to see you and DiMag, and you said 'Billy, don't write this, but I threw that Hodges a real hocker.' How could I, alone, write it? If I did, you and Joe would have denied it and clammed up on me forever."

"That Roe was throwin' it for them in '50," he said, meaning Preacher Roe of the Dodgers. "He later wrote about it. I used to load it up during a foul ball, when everybody looks up."

He got up now and walked slowly toward the barroom. When he came back he handed me his glove, still formed as it had been to fit his right hand, the dark brown, almost black leather cracked now.

"A Diz Trout model," he said.

"You ought to put oil on it," I said, as I handed it back.

"We're going to have it bronzed," Mitz said.

He sat down, and she stood up and began kneading his shoulders again.

"Them were good days in New York," he said. "We had a lot of fun."

"One day," she said, "he told Jon, 'Remember, if you're going to make it, you're going to have to work hard. And stay away from women.' Then we were going through some old things, and found a picture of Joe and Joe DiMaggio in Hawaii with these girls. So Jon took it to him, and said, 'What about this?'"

"I tortured a few in my day," he said.

"So you had your good days," she said, "and you should remember those."

"Yeah," he said, "and the young buck can play ball, too."

"Jon was playing over in Johnstown," she said, "and Joe used to tell this story of one he hit there."

"I hit one out 380 feet," he said.

"So Jon hit one out 440 feet," she said, "and Joe said, 'I'll never tell that story again.'"

"That was the end of that hit," he said.

"I have to get a loaf of bread," she said, walking out from behind the chair, "and where do I get a headlight? The low beam is out."

"In a garage," he said.

"But what one? The outside of the light is square."

"But the light is round," young Joe said. "Go to Mobil."

"I'll be back in a few minutes," she said.

"She don't know cars," Page said, "but she's got a hell of a brain. She works twelve, fourteen hours a day, Skip."

"She seems to be a fine woman," Skipper said.

"You can say that again," he said. "What beats me is that I can't hunt any more, and I've got them guns."

"What have you got?" Skipper said.

"I got a .320, a .406, and a .373 Magnum, and I can't use them."

"Didn't you once go on a bird hunting trip to Maine with Enos Slaughter and a couple of others?" I said.

"It was South Dakota," he said. "Huron. A guy had to be blind not to get fifty roosters."

"You were telling about it in the clubhouse one day," I said, "and Yogi was listening. You said, 'We were going after birds, and Slaughter had a cyst on his back, but it didn't make any difference to him. He went climbing through the brush and under those branches like it wasn't there.' And Yogi said, 'What the hell kind of a bird is a cyst?'"

"That's right," he said. " That was Yogi."

"With all you've been through," I said, "I've been thinking about that ballplayers' retirement plan. I've forgotten when that came in."

"We started it in '47," he said, "but it went back to '44. I know on the hospitalization they don't give you all of it, only 80 percent."

"But that's a big help."

"Hell, yes," he said, bringing his hand up to his neck again. "This thing cost $19,000."

Young Joe had turned on the TV again, for the American Football Conference playoff. We talked about the game against Boston on the next to last day of the season in '49. The Red Sox led the Yankees by one game in the standings, and were ahead, 4-1, in the second inning when he came in and held them the rest of the way until Johnny Lindell won it with a home run. Then the Yankees beat them again, to win the pennant on the last day.

"The good old days," he said, as we got up to leave. "I'm glad you came, and that you're looking good."

"And I'll call you now and then," I said, "to hear that you're feeling better."

"I was fifty-nine in October," he said.

"I know," I said.

He walked us out, after we had said good-bye to young

Joe, and closed the door behind him and stood, watching, under the overhang while we walked to the car. Darkness had come by now, and another car, its lights on, drove in and Mitz got out. We walked over and shook hands.

"I'm really pleased you two came," she said. "It's done a lot for him."

"You've done a lot for him," Skipper said.

"It's been a long time," she said, "since he's talked that much or sounded so well, or moved so well."

"I'm glad," I said.

"So any time you're nearby," she said, "stop in to see him again."

"We'd like to," I said.

As Skipper backed the car around I looked back. He was still standing under the overhang, under the pale overhead light, waving good-bye with his right hand.

"You know how pitchers are," Skipper said. "When they're talking, especially about pitching, they'll demonstrate with their pitching arm. He has to use his right arm."

"It was one of the great left arms," I said, "and it's a damn shame."

I had a terrible time trying to get to sleep that night. The Derry Sportsmen's Club was having its annual dinner dance in the ballroom of the motel, and it came up through the ventilating system and through the floor. The band must have played "Rock Around the Clock" a dozen times, but I would have had trouble sleeping anyway.

1976

William Brashler

≈

From The Bingo Long Traveling All-Stars and Motor Kings

When Leon Carter got to the mound the fans of the Louisville Ebony Aces applauded lightly. It was tradition for Leon to throw his first pitch without a team behind him. It would be a fastball, screaming down the center of the plate from a straight overhand motion after Leon had pawed and kicked his leg in the air like a stallion.

The leadoff hitter was a skinny second baseman, Cool Papa Blue. Cool Papa hit almost .400 last year and led his team, the Memphis Shots, to second place in the Southern Colored League. He would get Leon Carter's fastball invitation like anybody else. The home crowd stamped their feet on the wooden bleachers. The old men yelled, "C'mon, Cool Papa, hit the invite pitch."

Bingo Long crouched behind the plate. He watched Cool Papa Blue step into the batter's box, Blue's baggy pants blowing slightly against his legs, the green script letters spelling "Shots" spread from one arm to the other. "Whatayasay, Blue," Bingo said, and Cool Papa winked without looking down at him. Leon Carter waited on the mound, looking blankly at Bingo and Blue. Then the umpire motioned him on. Bingo gave no sign. He just raised his thick catcher's mitt, held it like a plate at Cool Papa's knees, and waited for Leon's kick.

The pitcher touched his cap, rubbed his hand across his chest, and grabbed the ball from his mitt to begin the pendulum motion of his windup. His left leg began to rise. Bingo dug in on his haunches behind the plate. Cool Papa drummed his fingers against the handle of the bat. Then Leon's right foot pushed against the pitching rubber, his right arm rose like a snake's head and spit out the white pellet. Cool Papa lashed at it. Bingo caught it like a pistol shot in the wet pocket of his mitt. A cheer went up from the fans. The game had begun. And the rest of the Ebony Aces trotted out to their positions.

ミ●

Yet there was nothing as sweet as watching Bingo take batting practice. He leaned into each pitch with his huge arms, whipping the bat around and cracking the ball. His usual blast was as high as it was far. At the peak of its ascent it hung in the sky like a dirigible about to burst, and then it lazily fell behind the fence. The kids in blue jeans and bare backs stood behind the backstop and winced each time Bingo smashed one. Some mimicked him, swinging an imaginary bat as he swung his, and then gazed off into the sky following the ball. They could feel the power, the icy connection stinging through them just as if they had swatted the ball like a fat bug and then circled the bases and heard the cheers. Bingo grinned at them, flexed the muscle in his right arm, and then fouled one straight back into the screen about head-high on the kids. It jolted the wires and sent them ducking and yelling.

1973

William Brashler

❧

From Josh Gibson, A Life in the Negro Leagues

His home runs were most often long drives, deep, not necessarily high but often so; or quick, smashing blows that flew off the bat and rushed out of the stadium. They were, in every sense of the word, "Ruthian," for Babe's considerable strength made so many of his home runs tape-measure clouts. Yet to so many who saw the way Josh hit them day in and day out, they were "Gibsonian," with a power and velocity equal to anything Ruth ever hit. The most memorable were to dead center field, a mark of perfect contact between bat and a ball at the precisely perfect instant. Yet he pulled as many to left, and nailed others into the right-field stands. Few people remember Josh's home runs as being restricted to any one field, and mention that they were similar only in the way they disappeared.

The stories go on and on. He hit so many, and so many saw them go. There are the tales about Josh hitting one out of sight on one afternoon only to have it reappear out of the sky the next day. Of course, the umpire said, "Yer out! Yes-

terday in Pittsburgh!" And there are the less apocryphal stories of games being stopped in mid-inning so the home team
could measure the blow. The mayor of Monessen, Pennsylvania, did it one day, arriving at a distance of 512 feet.

The most engaging stories are from teammates or opponents who remember what it was like to play with him each
day, and who saw the best of the Negro leagues and the
white leagues try to outfox him or fake him out, fool him or
overpower him.

Jack Marshall, who played most of his career with
Chicago's Negro teams but who hooked on with Josh during
the off-season or south of the border, remembers not a home
run but a line-drive single Josh hit in York, Pennsylvania,
one day. It shot off his bat at shortstop Willie Wells, one of
the Negro leagues' greatest shortstops, but Wells couldn't
do anything with it. The ball hit Wells' glove so hard that it
split the skin on his left hand. Wells, like most fielders of the
era who wore compact, short-fingered gloves, caught most
infield hits in the pocket of the glove and built up a tough,
callused palm. But Josh's drive went through his glove and,
said Marshall, "split the web of skin between his thumb and
his first finger right apart."

Marshall also vividly remembers one of Josh's "quick"
drives, one hit in Comiskey Park in Chicago. Comiskey was
a major-league stadium with long fences, and its center-field
wall was 435 feet from home plate. On it, about 8 feet off the
ground, were loudspeakers facing toward the field and about
20 inches in diameter. Josh hit a drive to straight-away center that to Marshall never seemed to rise, staying instead on
a straight line like a frozen rope. It struck a loudspeaker
dead center and stuck in it like an apple. The game was
stopped while a groundskeeper pried it free.

Jimmie Crutchfield played alongside Josh for five years
and against him for many more, and he can think of count-

less times that Josh left everyone in the stands wide-eyed. Crutchfield remembers a game against the Nashville Elite Giants which was played in front of a big crowd, including a complete minor-league team who made the game just to see Josh perform. The Elite Giants' manager was Candy Jim Taylor, who said before the game that he knew how to pitch Josh. Taylor insisted that Josh could not hit a sidewinder, a pitch fired from the third-base side of the mound. During a crucial time in the game, with Josh's team behind, Cool Papa Bell doubled, Crutchfield followed with a single, and Josh came up representing the go-ahead run. Taylor quickly stopped the game and went out to instruct his pitcher, Andrew Porter, to throw nothing but sidewinders. According to Crutchfield, Josh dug in at the plate and waited for his pitch. When he got it, a sidewinder coming at him and snaking for the outside of the plate, Josh stroked it. "I can see it now," said Jimmie. "It just went out of the park like the wind."

It seemed Josh hit best against the best, against tough Negro-league pitchers who faced him down and made him hit what they had. His tremendous home run in Yankee Stadium against the Lincoln Giants in September 1930, only months after he had joined the Grays at age eighteen, came during the heat of a tough series against Cornelius "Connie" Rector, one of the best Negro-league pitchers of the time. Cum Posey considered it one of the greatest hits of Josh's career, and one which came under enormous pressure.

Yankee Stadium, "the House That Ruth Built," brought out the best in Josh whenever he set foot inside the park. Against the New York Black Yankees (oddly enough, one of Negro baseball's weaker franchises throughout the years, even though it potentially had one of the biggest followings), Josh hit three homers one Sunday afternoon in the early 1930s. One of them, as Black Yankee shortstop Bill Yancey remembers, was another of Josh's unforgettable "quick" home runs. "He walloped three that day and one of them was the quickest home run I ever saw. It was out of the park before the outfielders could turn their heads to watch it. It landed behind the Yankee Stadium bullpen, some five hundred feet away. He didn't loft it, he shot it out of there."

Another of his Yankee Stadium clouts went to right field, landing in Tier 26. By all accounts, that was six tiers farther than one hit by Jimmie Foxx, a drive at that time considered the longest ever hit in those seats.

Other major-league parks were comparably assaulted. Cum Posey considered a Gibson home run to straight-away center field in Pittsburgh's Forbes Field as the longest ever hit there. Posey insisted that only Josh and John Beckwith, an awesome power hitter with a variety of teams in the 1920s, had ever popped one over the fence. One of Josh's blasts over the right-field wall in Cincinnati's Crosley Field was considered one of the longest ever hit there, and similarly branded was a home run in Cleveland's Municipal Stadium.

In Washington's Griffith Stadium, a ballpark in which Josh played many games later in his career, his home-run totals rivaled those of the entire major-league Washington Senator squad. That stadium was lined with twenty-foot-high walls covered with advertising. Once Josh hit a line drive against the right-field fence which slammed into a hot-dog sign, knocking paint and dust everywhere. A fan quickly yelled, "B'gosh! Josh knocked the mustard off that dog!"

1978

Roger Kahn

ह

From The Era

On April 22, a clear, cold day — the temperature never rose above 45 degrees — the Philadelphia Phillies came to Ebbets Field to start a three-game series. Ben Chapman, born in Tennessee and raised in Alabama, was the manager of the Phillies, a thick-browed, volatile character with a tumultuous history. He played outfield for the Yankees during the early 1930s, batting as high as .316 and stealing sixty-one bases in a single season. Like anyone else, he made bad plays from time to time and when he did, the fans at Yankee Stadium sometimes jeered. Most ballplayers ignore hoots. Chapman took a different route. Jeered by Yankee fans in the Bronx one day in 1932, he turned to the grandstand and shouted: "F-----g Jew bastards."

His intemperance persisted. Fans complained to the Yankee management, and at length, in 1936, the Yankees traded Chapman to Washington for another outfielder, Alvin "Jake"

Powell.[1] Chapman went from Washington to the Red Sox to the Indians to the White Sox, before dropping out of the major leagues. Late in World War II, when the military had claimed the best ballplayers — Greenberg, DiMaggio, Musial, Williams — Chapman signed with a weak Dodger team as a backup outfielder and sometime pitcher. The Phillies hired him to manage in 1945.

If Chapman disliked Jews, and he did dislike Jews, he hated "nigras." As the Dodger-Phillies game began, Chapman's strong, carrying drawl rose from the visiting dugout.

"Hey, you, there. Snowflake. Yeah, you. You heah me. When did they let you outa the jungle ...

"Hey, we doan need no niggers here ...

"Hey, black boy. You like white poontang, black boy? You like white pussy? Which one o' the white boys' wives are you f-----g tonight?"

Usually in baseball, even crude assaults give rise to back and forth banter. None was forthcoming in Ebbets Field that chilly April day. The Dodgers, southern and northern Dodgers, Dixie Walker and Carl Furillo, Pee Wee Reese and Spider Jorgensen, were shocked. Like Robinson, they sat in silence.

Lee Handley, Ben Chapman's third baseman, later made it a point to seek out Robinson. He said quietly, "I'm sorry. I want you to know that stuff doesn't go for me." Handley was the first opposing major-leaguer to treat Robinson as a man.

Robinson remembered Lee Handley, out of Clarion, Iowa, for the rest of his life. But he could no more respond to

---

[1] Powell himself was no peony. Off season, he told reporters at his first Yankee press conference, he worked as a cop in Toledo, Ohio. When asked specifically what he did on the Toledo police force, Powell told the New York press: "I hit niggers over the head with my nightstick."

Handley at the time than he could respond to Ben Chapman. He thought of the many times he had been told that he had to turn the other cheek. But, Robinson asked himself, do I really have to live a sermon?

Years later, when we were working up a story on bigotry for *Our Sports,* a magazine in which he had invested, Robinson recalled his reactions to Ben Chapman in the Golgotha of that clear, cold April day.

"I don't remember everything they shouted. Probably just as well. My wife, Rae, she's into psychology. She says that some things that are too upsetting, you make yourself forget."

Although Robinson could not or would not recount all that he heard, he vividly remembered his emotions. "All my life I've been a proud guy. I won't sit in the back of a bus. If you call me nigger or boy, I want to tear your throat out. I'm a proud guy.

"So there I am in Brooklyn, which is supposed to be the Promised Land, and I'm hearing the worst garbage I ever heard in my whole life, counting the streets, counting the army, but I've sworn to Mr. Rickey that I won't fight back.

"It's Chapman and some of the Phillies ballplayers, and I set my face and I say goddamn, I'm supposed to ignore 'em and just play ball.

"So I play ball, but they don't stop. Jungle bunny. Snowflake. I start breathing hard. I'm just playing ball. I'm doing my job. I'm a good ballplayer. Deep down, I've been thinking, people will see I'm a good ballplayer and they'll see I'm black and they'll put that together. A black guy's a good ballplayer. A black guy can be a good guy.

"But that's not happening. What do the Phillies want from me? What did I ever do to them? What does Mr. Rickey want? I'm in great shape. I'm playing hard. I'm not sassing anybody. What the hell does everybody want from me?

"All of a sudden I thought, the hell with this. This isn't me. They're making me be some crazy pacifist black freak. Hell, no. Hell, no. I'm going back to being myself. Right now. I'm going into the Phillie dugout and grab one of those white sons of bitches and smash his f-----g teeth and walk away. Walk away from this ballpark. Walk away from baseball.

"I thought some more. This didn't take as long in my head as it takes to tell you, Rog. I thought of Mr. Rickey and Rae and my baby son. Standing on that ballfield in Brooklyn, standing still, I had come to a crossroads.

"For a second I felt, this is it. I'm cracking up.

"But wait, wait, wait. Am I gonna give Ben Chapman that satisfaction . . ."

In the eighth inning Robinson singled up the middle. Then he stole second base. When Andy Seminick's throw bounced into center field, Robinson ran on to third. Gene Hermanski singled to right. That was the run. There weren't any more. The Dodgers defeated the Phillies, 1 to 0, on Robinson's run.

Robinson took the subway back to the McAlpin Hotel on 34th Street in Manhattan, where he lived while looking for an apartment. Rachel cooked dinner on an electric hot plate. The baby, Jack Roosevelt Robinson, Jr., had a cold and the couple stayed up much of the night trying to help their child sleep.

At Ebbets Field the next day, Robinson walked up to bat in the first inning feeling better than he had the day before.

"Hey, Jungle Bunny," Ben Chapman shouted. "You go out and get yo-sef some white pussy last night?"

&

Stanky and a few other ballplayers told newspapermen what was going on. Branch Rickey, informed by his new manager, Burt Shotton, telephoned the commissioner, Happy Chandler. Something had to be done, Rickey said, in the name of decency.

Chandler had suspended Leo Durocher for a year, ostensibly for living loosely. What punishment, then, would be appropriate for William Benjamin Chapman, Klansman without a hood?

Chandler considered at length. Then he ordered Chapman to grant an interview to Wendell Smith, a congenial black sportswriter for the black newspaper the *Pittsburgh Courier*.

No suspension. Not even a fine. Just a suggestion that Chapman ease up and an order that he spend one hour in civil conversation with a Negro.

Dan Parker wrote a column in the *Daily Mirror* criticizing Chapman's "guttersnipe" language. But generally the press persisted in its belligerent neutrality. This account, from The *Sporting News* of May 7, 1947, is characteristic:

> Jackie Robinson's position in the major leagues and the manner in which he will be treated by the Philadelphia Phillies was clarified in a straight from the shoulder interview from Ben Chapman...
>
> "We treat Robinson the same as we do Hank Greenberg of the Pirates, Clint Hartung of the Giants, Connie Ryan of the Braves," Chapman said.
>
> "When I came into the big leagues, pitchers threw at me, dusted me off, pegged at my head, my legs. I was dangerous.
>
> "Robinson can run. He can bunt. He's dangerous.
>
> "When I came into the league, they wanted to see if I would lose my temper and forget to play ball. They tried to break my morale. They played baseball for keeps. That's the way we're going to play with Robinson.
>
> "If Robinson has the stuff, he'll be accepted in baseball, the same as the Sullivans and the Grodzickis. All I expect him to do is prove it. Let's get the chips off our shoulders and play ball."

I mean to suggest that at this point, early in the 1947 season, the issue of Robinson's success — the question of integrated baseball — was seriously in doubt. (So, indeed, was Robinson's mental health.) Oddly, his most vociferous ballfield supporter at that time was Eddie Stanky, the second baseman from Philadelphia who had moved to Mobile and who years later himself needled Robinson in unpleasant ways. But in May 1947 something deep and good was touched within Eddie Stanky, a combative, thin-lipped, verbal ballplayer with limited physical skills and limitless fire. "Those guys [the Phillies] are a disgrace," Stanky told the New York newspapermen. "They know Robinson can't fight back. There isn't one of them who has the guts of a louse." After Chapman's behavior moved Stanky to Jackie Robinson's side, other Dodgers, notably Pee Wee Reese, quickly followed. Some — Bobby Bragan, Hugh Casey, Cookie Lavagetto, and Dixie Walker — did not.

The issue still was in doubt. Herb Pennock, the general manager of the Phillies, had been the leading left-handed pitcher on the 1927 New York Yankees, a team that remains the benchmark of baseball excellence. Tall, lean, dignified, Pennock was nicknamed "The Squire of Kennett Square," after the Pennsylvania town where he was born.

The Dodgers were scheduled to begin a series in Philadelphia on May 9 and Pennock telephoned Branch Rickey to impose conditions. "You just can't bring the nigger here with the rest of your team, Branch," Pennock said. "We're not ready for that sort of thing yet in Philadelphia. We won't be able to take the field [at Shibe Park] against your Brooklyn team, if that boy is in uniform."

Major-league rules require that both sides field a team for every scheduled game. Should one side fail to appear, the other team is awarded victory by forfeit. The score of a forfeit is recorded as 9 to 0.

"Very well, Herbert," Rickey said, "if you don't field a team and we must claim the game, 9 to 0, we will do just that, I assure you."

Rickey hung up. Pennock was not through making mischief. When the Dodgers arrived at the 30th Street Station in Philadelphia and took taxis to the Benjamin Franklin Hotel on the morning of May 9, they were turned away in the lobby. Pennock and his employers had spoken to the hotel owners. The hotel would take "no ballclub nigras." Harold Parrott, the Dodgers' toothy traveling secretary, had to shuttle about Philadelphia for hours before he found a hotel — the Warwick — willing to accommodate the team. Until then, the Dodgers were considering commuting for the series. Recalling that Philadelphia story, Parrott summed up: "Talk about brotherly love."

Rickey, not satisfied with Ben Chapman's feathery reprimand, continued to press Commissioner Chandler for significant action. Chandler responded by hiring Jack Demoise, a former FBI agent, to travel the National League "and look for troublemakers." Then, finally, the commissioner telephoned Pennock. "If you move in on Robinson," Chandler said, "I'll move in on you."

Chapman himself was slow recognizing the new thrust of things. Gene Hermanski, a Dodger outfielder for seven seasons, is white-haired now, but so vigorous and feisty in his seventies that someone describes him as a "walking advertisement against Grecian Formula" (a popular over-the-counter product that turns white hair dark). Hermanski, who was born in Pittsfield, Massachusetts, and resides in central New Jersey, says, as so many old Dodgers do, "Jackie Robinson was a great man."

"Philadelphia, Gene," I say. "Do you remember Philadelphia, 1947?"

Hermanski's eyes light. "That bastard Chapman." Hermanski moves backward on wings of memory. His eyes are burning now.

In Philadelphia, first game there, during pregame warm-ups, Chapman started shouting again. But not at Robinson this time. "Hey, Pee Wee," Chapman yelled. "Yeah, you. Reese. How ya like playin' with a f----n' nigger?"

Reese ignored Chapman, who shouted the question again. And yet a third time.

Reese stopped picking up ground balls and jogged over to Robinson at first base. Then, staring into the Philadelphia dugout, Reese put an arm around Jackie Robinson's shoulders.

"Pee Wee didn't say a word," Gene Hermanski remembers. "But Chapman had his answer."

1993

Red Smith

﷯

From Strawberries in the Wintertime

In the scene that doesn't fade, the Brooklyn Dodgers are tied with the Phillies in the bottom of the 12th inning. It is 6 p.m. on an October Sunday, but the gloom in Philadelphia's Shibe Park is only partly due to oncoming evening. The Dodgers, champions-elect in August, have frittered away a lead of 13½ games, and there is bitterness in the dusk of this last day of the 1951 baseball season. Two days ago, the New York Giants drew even with Brooklyn in the pennant race. Two hours ago, the numbers went up on the scoreboard: New York 3, Boston 2. The pennant belongs to the Giants unless the Dodgers can snatch it back.

With two out and the bases full of Phillies, Eddie Waitkus smashes a low, malevolent drive toward center field. The ball is a blur passing second base, difficult to follow in the half-light, impossible to catch. Jackie Robinson catches it. He flings himself headlong at right angles to the flight of the ball, for an instant his body is suspended in midair, then somehow the outstretched glove intercepts the ball inches off the ground.

He falls heavily, the crash drives an elbow into his side, he collapses. But the Phillies are out, the score is still tied.

Now it is the 14th inning. It is too dark to play baseball, but the rules forbid turning on lights for a game begun at 2 o'clock. Pee Wee Reese pops up. So does Duke Snider. Robin Roberts throws a ball and a strike to Robinson. Jackie hits the next pitch upstairs in left field for the run that sets up baseball's most memorable playoff.

That was the day that popped into mind when word came yesterday that Jack Roosevelt Robinson had died at 53. Of all the pictures he left upon memory, the one that will always flash back first shows him stretched at full length in the insubstantial twilight, the unconquerable doing the impossible.

The word for Jackie Robinson is "unconquerable." In *The Boys of Summer*, Roger Kahn sums it up: "In two seasons, 1962 and 1965, Maury Wills stole more bases than Robinson did in all of a 10-year career. Ted Williams' lifetime batting average, .344, is two points higher than Robinson's best for any season. Robinson never hit 20 home runs in a year, never batted in 125 runs. Stan Musial consistently scored more often. Having said those things, one has not said much because troops of people who were there believe that in his prime Jackie Robinson was a better ballplayer than any of the others."

Another picture comes back. Robinson has taken a lead off first base and he crouches, facing the pitcher, feet fairly wide apart, knees bent, hands held well out from his sides to help him balance, teetering on the balls of his feet. Would he be running? His average was 20 stolen bases a year and Bugs Baer wrote that "John McGraw demanded more than that from the baseball writers."

Yet he was the only base runner of his time who could bring a game to a stop just by getting on base. When he walked to first, all other action ceased. For Robinson, television introduced the split screen so the viewer at home as well as the fan in the park could watch both the runner on first and the pitcher standing irresolute, wishing he didn't have to throw.

Jackie Robinson established the black man's right to play second base. He fought for the black man's right to a place in the white community, and he never lost sight of that goal. After he left baseball, almost everything he did was directed toward that goal. He was involved in foundation of the Freedom National Banks. He tried to get an insurance company started with black capital and when be died he was head of a construction company building housing for blacks. Years ago a friend, talking of the needs of blacks, said "good schooling comes first."

"No," Jackie said, "housing is the first thing. Unless he's got a home he wants to come back to, it doesn't matter what kind of school be goes to."

There was anger in him and when he was a young man be tended to raise his falsetto voice. "But my demands were modest enough," he said, and he spoke the truth. The very last demand he made publicly was delivered in the mildest of terms during the World Series just concluded. There was a ceremony in Cincinnati saluting him for his work in drug addiction and in his response he mentioned a wish that he could look down to third base and see a black manager on the coaching line.

Seeing him in Cincinnati recalled the Dylan Thomas line that Roger Kahn borrowed for a title: "I see the boys of summer in their ruin." At 53 Jackie was sick of body, white of hair. He had survived one heart attack, he had diabetes and high blood-pressure and he was going blind as a result of retinal bleeding in spite of efforts to cauterize the ruptured blood vessels with laser beams. With him were his wife, Rachel, their son, David, and daughter, Sharon. Everybody was remembering Jack Jr., an addict who beat the heroin habit and died at 24 in an auto accident.

"I've lost the sight in one eye," Jackie had told Kahn a day or so earlier, "but they think they can save the other. I've got nothing to complain about."

1974

Roger Angell

ₑ

From Five Seasons

There was another moment on that same bright Sunday — a moment before the game, which only took on meaning a few days later. In a brief ceremony at the mound, Commissioner Bowie Kuhn presented an award to Jackie Robinson, honoring him for his work in combating drug addiction, and celebrating his arrival, twenty-five years before, as a the first black man in the major leagues. Robinson responded, his thin, high voice barely reaching us over the loudspeakers. He was glad to see some of his old Brooklyn friends there — Pee Wee Reese, Joe Black, Red Barber. He introduced his family. He ended by saying that it would be nice to see a black manager standing in the third-base coach's box someday soon. There were handshakes and applause, the party walked away, the microphones were taken down. I had seen Jackie for a minute or two in the tunnel behind home plate — a frail, white-haired old man, with a black raincoat buttoned up to his chin. I remembered at that moment a baseball scene that I had witnessed more than twenty years earlier — a scene that came back to me the following week, when I read about Robinson's sudden death. It was something that had happened during an insignificant weekday game between the Giants and the Dodgers back in the 1950s. Robinson, by then an established star, was playing third base that afternoon, and during the game something happened that drove him suddenly and totally mad. I was sitting close to him, just behind third, but I had no idea what brought on the outburst. It might have been a remark from the stands or from one of the dugouts; it was nothing that happened on the field. Without warning, Robinson began shouting imprecations, obscenities, curses. His voice was piercing, his face distorted with passion. The players on both teams looked at each other, uncomprehending. The Giants' third-base coach walked over to murmur a question, and Robinson directed his screams at him. The umpire at third did the same thing, and then turned away with a puzzled, embarrassed shrug. In time, the outburst stopped and the game went on. It had been nothing, a moment's aberration, but it seemed to suggest what can happen to a man who has been used, who has been made into a symbol and a public sacrifice. The moment became an event — something to remember along with the innumerable triumphs and joys and the sense of pride and redress that Jackie Robinson brought to us all back then. After that moment, I knew that we had asked him to do too much for us. None of it — probably not a day of it — was easy for him.

1977

Jim Langford

From The Game is Never Over

In this era of domed stadia, expansive waterfront parks, artificial turf, and heavy night schedules, Wrigley Field is a splendid anomaly. It sits, uncovered, in the midst of an old neighborhood in north Chicago. Both its grass and its lighting system are natural. Its exterior and interior each betray the fact that it has been here for sixty-six years and counting. Yet despite its lack of spatial largesse and bright colors, it looks more like a baseball park than do those giant structures built to house football as conveniently as baseball.

Inside, one feels pleasure at the beauty of the green grass, the vines covering the outfield walls, the symmetry of the left- and right-field bleachers as they sweep away from the large scoreboard in center. There is also a strong sense that your presence is part of what will take place here today. The seats are close enough to the field that shouts of encouragement or dismay will be heard and, if at all possible, heeded.

For Wrigley Field is more than a park with a charm all

its own; it is more than functional antique. Wrigley Field is a shrine to the endurance and resilience of hope. It is a witness to the fact that teams do not necessarily have to win pennants to inspire and keep allegiance. The Cubs have never had to be an itinerant team moving from city to city, staying only until the novelty of winning has worn off. The Cubs have been in Chicago since 1876, the year the National League was founded. And Wrigley Field has been their home since 1916, through good times and bad. There is something uniquely familial, American, traditional about Wrigley Field, something shared by no other ballpark in the country, save perhaps Fenway Park in Boston and Comiskey Park on the south side of Chicago.

Its distinction as the only major league stadium without lights indicates not merely the traditional wisdom that baseball was meant to be played in the sun, but also reflects an admirable sense of responsibility to one's neighbors. Night baseball would bring with it crowds and cars, shouts and sirens, denying the neighboring families their right to evenings of peace and quiet. As Philip K. Wrigley put it: "It's just self-protection, as I see it, to maintain good relations with our neighbors. Imagine night games in that residential neighborhood and with the noise, confusion, traffic and late hours, we'd soon lose our rating as a good neighbor." Pressured in the early sixties to install lights as a way of combating declining attendance, Mr. Wrigley answered with true insight, "It's not night baseball we need, it's winning baseball." Record attendance in the near-pennant years of the late sixties bore out the truth of what he said.

But it is not only the neighbors of Wrigley Field who appreciate the absence of lights at the park. Scores of Cub players have said how much they prefer to play in the daylight. None has said it better than longtime Cub player, manager, and executive, Charlie Grimm: "In my time you could tell a ballplayer by his clear, sharp eyes and his ruddy skin. If things keep going in the night ball trend the modern ballplayer can be identified by the thick-lensed glasses he wears and his squint when he ventures out into the sun."

Wrigley Field is, in fact, a sign of continuity to the way baseball was played even before Charlie Grimm's time. The park was built in the teen years of this century and is now in its seventh decade of continuous service. Its early contemporaries in National League cities — Forbes Field in Pittsburgh, Crosley Field in Cincinnati, Shibe Park in Philadelphia, Braves Field in Boston, the Polo Grounds in New York, Ebbets Field in Brooklyn, and Sportsman's Park in St. Louis — are all gone or retired now. Only Wrigley Field remains. So what? Nothing, except that there is a special sense of history in this field that you cannot find elsewhere. You cannot see the Reds play today in the same park where Johnny Vander Meer pitched successive no-hitters on June 11 and June 15, 1938. The Polo Grounds and Ebbets Field are parking lots now, and there is no way to see for oneself where Bobby Thomson hit his dramatic homer off Ralph Branca to win the pennant for the Giants in 1951, or where Willie Mays made his spectacular catch of Vic Wertz's long drive in the 1954 World Series, or where Jackie Robinson first took up his station at second base and broke the color line that had kept black players out of the big leagues. And so on through hundreds of memorable moments in baseball now deprived of their historical settings.

But you can still come to Wrigley Field and be in a park where all the greatest stars in the National League since 1916 have played and where the American League champions met the Cubs in five World Series. Sample a few of the names: Grover Cleveland Alexander, Rogers Hornsby, Honus

Wagner, Frankie Frisch, Mel Ott, the Waner brothers, Dizzy Dean, Bill Terry, Gabby Hartnett, Kiki Cuyler. Or, for that matter, Babe Ruth, Lou Gehrig, Bill Dickey, Mickey Cochrane, Joe DiMaggio, Red Ruffing, Jimmy Foxx, and Hank Greenberg. In fact, a majority of those honored in the Baseball Hall of Fame came to this park, walked through its gates, dressed in its innards, leaned on it bricks, and played the game as only they could.

It was in this very park that the greatest pitching duel of all time took place. On May 2, 1917, Fred Toney, a right-hander for the Cincinnati Reds, went against Cub southpaw Jim "Hippo" Vaughn. There was not a single hit on either side for nine innings. In the tenth frame, with one out, Cincinnati's Larry Kopf singled between Fred Merkle and Larry Doyle for the game's first hit. Cy Williams of the Cubs then proceeded to muff Hal Chase's pop fly (yes, Virginia, it was happening even back then), and Kopf raced to third. Up came the fabled Jim Thorpe. He hit a high bounder in front of the plate. Hippo Vaughn came pounding in to get it and threw to the plate, but catcher Art Wilson was looking elsewhere, missed the ball, and a run scored. Toney retired the Cubs in order in the tenth to preserve his no-hitter and take the 1-0 win.

Wrigley Field was the home of Hack Wilson in 1930 when he hit 56 home runs and drove in 190 runs. It was at Wrigley Field in 1932 that Babe Ruth is supposed to have pointed to the spot where he would hit Charlie Root's next pitch and then did so. And it was here in 1938 that Gabby Hartnett hit his famous "homer in the gloaming" with two outs in the ninth to take the pennant from the Pirates and give it to the Cubs. The list of thrills could go on and on to include a perfect game by Sandy Koufax, a near perfect game by Milt Pappas, and another by Don Cardwell, a dramatic no-hitter by Sam Jones, innumerable homers by Ernie Banks, and hundreds of those late-inning rallies for which the Cubs are justly famous.

And there are other memories, too, less pleasant ones.

Long-suffering Cub fans still exist who can point you to the approximate section of brick behind first base that served as backstop for erratic throws from Roy Smalley, Andre Rogers, and Robert Pena. Some can still see the ghosts of Cub outfielders dropping fly balls and of Cub catchers racking up passed balls, dodging wild pitches, or trying in vain to nail Maury Wills or Lou Brock at second, even on a pitchout.

But Wrigley Field has another kind of history about it, too. It is a stage on which thousands of dramas have played. Even if a majority of the games were not dramatic, tension-filled battles, each one meant something in the lives of the players, managers, coaches, and umpires who participated. In the ebb and flow of careers, every game was a benchmark of sorts. Hundreds of rookies played their first major-league game here. One can only imagine the emotions experienced by a young athlete the first time he puts on a major-league uniform and walks down the passageway to the field. As a newcomer, he is self-conscious. He is anxious to look good, even the way he walks and jogs and plays catch. He looks for signs of acceptance from the veterans, hoping that they have not forgotten what their first day was like. And hundreds of players put on the uniform for the last time here, experiencing that special kind of pain inflicted by the knowledge that their bodies can no longer compete against those more youthful and that not even cunning can compensate for tired muscles and slowed reflexes. Their turn is up; their names will not again be penciled into the starting lineup.

Dreams have been realized and dashed in this park. Some

players were here only long enough to taste what it is like and then, judged to be in need of more seasoning, were sent away never to make it back. Others came to stay. Of these, some never lost the thrill of coming onto this field to play before its fans. Listen to Ernie Banks: "Look at those people. It's just like Ebbets Field. I think baseball is meant for small parks like this. It's a personal game. You've got to feel close, get involved. These people would sleep here if they could. So would I."

As Ernie suggests, Wrigley Field not only holds a special place in the lives of those who played here, it is also a locus of personal memories for the millions of people who have been here as fans. It is not simply a matter of recalling record-breaking performances witnessed here. The game itself is only part of the experience. The rest is a whole array of memories: recollections of being at Wrigley Field years ago with a now-deceased parent or loved one or of sharing the experience with one's own children for the first time. Few who have been to Wrigley Field forget the sights and sounds of the park, the players and the fans. The simple fact is that the park itself has an important role in the creation of that awesome steadfastness of Cub fans. It is a personal park, a vital link to the glory days of the past and to traditions that find new manifestations with each decade.

In the forties, fans had several years to follow the strange career of Lou Novikoff, the "Mad Russian," who, though the most fearsome hitter in minor-league history, never came to stay in four tries with the Cubs. As sportswriter Warren Brown describes Novikoff, no one ever claimed that he was a fielding genius. According to Brown, "The vines which decorated the walls of Wrigley Field were a constant source of worry to him. When a ball was hit over his head, the Mad Russian would back up so far, and no farther. More often than not, the ball recoiling from the wall bounded past him and in toward the infield with the Mad Russian in hot pursuit." Manager Charlie Grimm tried everything he could think of to cure Novikoff's fear of the vines. Grimm brought in samples of goldenrod to prove that the vines were not goldenrod and not likely to give Lou a case of hay fever. But that didn't work. Next Grimm demonstrated that the vines weren't poison ivy either. He pulled some off the wall, rubbed it over his face and hands and even chewed on a couple of leaves. But to no avail: the Mad Russian still stopped cold whenever he moved near the wall. Perhaps Lou's real allergy was to the solid bricks that were cleverly concealed by the vines. We may never know. The fact remains that Lou was a colorful character, and Cub fans adopted him, warts and all.

But the fans had later favorites who did better for them. In the fifties, the "bleacher bums" showered Hank Sauer with packages of Beech-Nut, his favorite chewing tobacco, as a way of saying thanks for the homers he hit into their midst. In the sixties, their shouts of "ole!" transformed Adolfo Phillips, if only briefly, into a stellar outfielder. Their favorite for 1980: Dave Kingman.

Cub players and members of opposing teams as well have often marveled at the devotion of Wrigley Field's patrons. And no one has ever accused Cub fans of being unknowing or uncritical. You can ask anyone in the bleachers what the Cubs need to become a winner, and he will tell you as astutely as any seasoned scout or general manager could. At least part of the explanation of the Cub phenomenon is the fact that the Wrigleys have always maintained the park with the comfort of the fans as a high priority. Over the years many interesting experiments have been made with the fans in mind. In 1955, a small section of the left-field grandstand was equipped with loudspeakers to provide the fans with the audio portion of Jack Brickhouse's telecast of the games. A year later a "speed walk" was installed to move thousands of fans from the ground floor to the upper deck. And a flag-signaling system was invented to accommodate those fans who hadn't been able to make it to the game; the blue "W" flag or white "L" flag gave them the day's results as they drove past the park.

Of course, the very mention of flag calls to mind for all Cub fans the wonderful aspect of chance which plays into every game at Wrigley Field. The park's proximity to Lake Michigan invites the winds that can determine to a large extent whether the game today will be a home run derby or a pitcher's duel. When the wind is blowing out, no lead is safe. When it is blowing in, powerful drives are harnessed and fall harmlessly into outfielder's gloves. Still, Wrigley Field's wind is not the gale of San Francisco's Candlestick Park; it can turn a fly ball into a home run or a home run into a fly out, but it does not threaten to blow the players off the field.

Wrigley Field is regarded as a hitter's park but not because there are short fences down the line. No "cheap" home runs are hit here. It is 355 feet from home plate to the wall in left field, and 353 feet to the wall in right. But unlike the newer parks, the wall here deepens only gradually and at its furthest extension it reaches 400 feet in dead center field. The power alleys in left-center and right-center are more reachable here than in most parks around the league. One other factor helps the batter. The stands are so close to the field that foul flies caught in other parks are out of play in Wrigley Field, thus giving the hitter another chance to get on base. Still, Ferguson Jenkins won twenty or more games six seasons in succession as a Cub, proving that a pitcher with good stuff can win here with consistency.

⋰⋱

Since the Cubs first moved to Wrigley Field in 1916, more than 56 million people have been there to cheer, to plead, and above all, to be loyal. In stiff collars and straw hats, baggy pants and bobby socks, Bermuda shorts and polo shirts, generations of fans have come to Wrigley Field to root for the Cubs. And they are still there. The fashions change, but the fans remain. Come to the field on a day when the Cubs are losing and, with two outs in the ninth, look around. There they sit. Complaining, but alert. Frustrated, but attentive. Dejected, yet happy. For Cub fans know, together, sitting there in that wonderful green field, the game is never over. Never.

1980

Pete Hamill

୬

From A Drinking Life

In the streets, we still played the now
forgotten games of the New York summers. Stickball was
the supreme game, a kind of tabloid version of baseball,
played with a broom handle as a bat and a pink rubber ball
manufactured by the A.G. Spalding Co. In every street in New
York, this ball was called a spaldeen. The spaldeens had vanished during the war and the game was played for a while
with hairy tennis balls, until even they had disappeared. But
coming home from Fox Lair Camp, I felt a special excitement
spreading through the neighborhood: *Spaldeens are back!*

From out of Unbeatable Joe's and Rattigan's and the
other bars, the men and the veterans came piling into the
streets again, taking our bats, once more playing the city's
greatest game, whacking spaldeens past trolley cars and over
rooftops, running bases on heat-softened tar, making impossible catches, dodging trolley cars and trucks, almost
delirious with joy. The war was over. The fucking war was
finally over.

Stickball ruled us. On Saturday mornings, the older guys played big games against visitors from other neighborhoods or went off themselves to play beyond our frontiers. *Money game!* someone would shout, and suddenly we were all moving to the appointed court and great noisy fiesta of the stickball morning. The players drank beer from cardboard containers on the sidelines and ate hero sandwiches and smoked cigarettes. They were cheered by neighbors, girlfriends, wives, and kids. And standing on the sidelines during those first games were the veterans, holding the spaldeens, bouncing them, smelling them in an almost sacramental way.

The men played on summer weekends; we kids played every day. There were still very few cars on the streets in that year after the war, so the "court" was always perfectly drawn, with sewer plates marking home and second base, while first and third were chalked against the curbs. The rules were settled before each game: one strike and you were out; off the factory wall or off a passing trolley car was a "hindoo" — which meant the play didn't count. The great hitters could hit the ball at least "three sewers," and it was said of Paulie McAleer of the Shamrock Boys that he once hit a ball an incredible five sewers. In memory, the games seem continuous and the days longer, richer, denser, and emptier than any others in my life. We did nothing and we did everything. You would wake, the radio playing, the rooms thick with the closed heat (and sometimes the sour smell of drink), grab something to eat — bread and butter covered with sugar, a piece of toast — and then race down the stairs, to burst into the streets. On a perfect Saturday in August, Twelfth Street would be wet from the water wagon, the air fresh, nobody else around, the tenements brooding in Edward Hopper light, and then a door would open and Billy

Rossiter would appear with the bat and the spaldeen, and that was all we needed. We'd play off the factory walls until the others came down; we'd play ten hits apiece until there were enough players to choose up sides. And then we'd play until dark.

1994

Larry King

࣒

On Billy Cox

Billy Cox was flat-out-hands-down-no-doubt-about-it my favorite all-time ballplayer. I saw better players than Cox at bat. Stan Musial was an artist with the wood. I saw better all-around players than Cox. Willie Mays was not only in a class by himself, he had the whole school. But for me, for my taste in baseball, no one touched my heart more than the diminutive third baseman, the best ever to field that position.

I became a Dodger fan at the age of ten in 1944, living in Brooklyn, New York. Cox became a Dodger in 1948, arriving from Pittsburgh along with pitcher Preacher Roe in one of the great one-sided deals of all-time. Gene Mauch, believe it or not, was also included in that arrangement, and Brooklyn sent Dixie Walker and pitchers Hal Gregg and Vic Lombardi to the Bucs. Had not Walker been such a vocal opponent of Jackie Robinson's color, the deal would never have come off. Later Dixie would tell me how much he regretted his own thinking; but I would thank him for giving me the joy of seeing Billy Cox play third on a daily basis.

He was originally a shortstop, but Pee Wee Reese owned short so manager Leo Durocher and then Burt Shotten, who came in as manager when Leo was suspended, put Cox on third. And magic happened. I mean it, absolute magic. He would hold his beat-up old Davega-type mitt, which couldn't have cost twenty bucks, in his right hand before each pitch was delivered. He would slip it slowly on his left hand as the ball came to the plate. He never crouched down in that typical infielder stance. He stood, almost casually, awaiting whatever was to happen. When the ball came to third, he invariably caught it. To his left, a master. To his right, like no one before or since. And that arm. That incredible, unbelievable arm. He threw the ball sidearm like a whiplash. Often he would hold it awhile before pegging it over to first just to keep things interesting.

He could hit in the clutch, batting a career .262; he hit .291 on the 1953 Dodgers, with 10 home runs.

But statistics are not the Billy Cox story. You had to see him, folks. I can still see Cox coming in on a bunt and that whiplike throw, literally in one motion. I've never seen anyone do it with that fluid grace. He would backhand a shot over third, then literally read the baseball before throwing. I can't remember an error.

I remember being at a spring training game in Miami in 1964. The Mets were playing the Orioles, and before the game Met manager Casey Stengel was holding forth in the dugout. Brooks Robinson came strolling by to get a bat and go up to take some batting practice. Casey yelled out, "You are the second-greatest third baseman who ever lived."

Brooks stopped in his tracks and walked over to the Met dugout. "Who's the best?" he asked.

Casey said quickly, "Number three. Used to play in Brooklyn. He had a better arm than you, Brooksie, a better arm.

There was nobody like him. But don't feel badly. You're the second-best and he was in a world all his own."

In my humble, childlike way, I tried to be Billy Cox. I wore number 3 whenever I had the chance. I tried to ape the way he walked. I knew he was a sullen, noncommunicative type, caused by malaria during World War II, so I never approached him for an autograph. I was scared. I was in awe. I still am. Just the mention of his name brings chills up and down my spine. Billy Cox. Third base. I was there — and you can look it up....

1990

Roger Towne and Phil Dusenberry

ঌ

From The Natural

The gate to the bullpen opens and YOUNGBERRY trots onto the field, a lean, golden-haired youngster.

SPORTSCASTER (V.O.)

Wicket is sending for his top reliever, rookie Herman Youngberry to pitch. A farmtown boy from Iowa with a blinding fastball...

On Youngberry and Wicket on mound

WICKET

All right. He's just out of a ladies hospital. He could keel over any second. Just hit the strike zone and we can all go home.

The confab breaks up, leaving Youngberry alone to warm up.

INT. PRESS BOX — MAX MERCY

CAMERA PULLS IN on a cartoon of Roy swinging blindly. The caption reads: "GOAT OF THE GAME."

ON YOUNGBERRY — SET

with great determination, he goes to his stretch and delivers.

Roy swings, connecting dangerously and lifting the ball foul over the right-field stands.

With a CRASH it hits Max Mercy's Press Box window. A loud shattering of glass resounds through the stadium. The players and crowd BUZZ in amazement at the sight of Max standing in the gaping jaws of jagged glass.

Youngberry, bristling with confidence, rears back, strides forward and uncorks the pitch.

Roys swings and misses. The crowd heaves a great sigh of disillusionment.

SPORTSCASTER (V.O.)

...Youngberry just one strike away from victory as the tension becomes unbearable.

Youngberry is looking in at Roy. He winds and delivers. Roy takes a whirling cut at it, meeting it squarely. The ball sails out in a low arc toward left as the runners go, but the third base umpire calls it, "FOUL!"

SLO-MO capturing the fractured halves of Wonderboy as they sail down to the ground.

The crowd moans horribly.

AT THE KNIGHTS DUGOUT

heads drop in disappointment. Pop looks catatonic.

Roy looks on for a long moment. Bobby runs out and gathers in the splintered halves of Wonderboy. He returns dutifully back to Roy.

ROY
(indicating the bat rack)

Pick me a winner, Bobby.

Bobby trots back to the bat rack. He lays Wonderboy down on the grass. He surveys the rack — hesitates, then pulls out a bat.

THE SANDLOT GAME

ON BOBBY

handing Roy the bat. Roy looks at it and at Bobby, then turns toward the batter's box. He grips the bat in his two hands, stopping for a long moment to reflect. Now we NOTICE blood just beginning to seep through Roy's shirt.

UMPIRE
(breaking in)

Hobbs? You Okay, fella?

Roy re-sets himself in the box with the new bat.

ROY

Let's play ball.

UMPIRE

Awright, that's what we're here for.

Roy sets the bat on his shoulder. An eerie silence has pervaded the stadium in the wake of Wonderboy's demise. Youngberry has a sneer on his face as he goes to his motion and — reaching back for something extra — releases the pitch.

CLOSE AT ROY with a seething fury, he swings — violently and perfectly — the ball exploding off his bat.

The Knights bench bolts to its feet.

The crowd, electrified; a frenzied reverberate scream.

The ball, a white blur aiming straight for the lights of the stadium roof. CRASH! One light goes. Then in a chain reaction, they all start to go — pop! pop! pop! — like a giant short circuit.

THE TOWER

The Judge and Gus turn ashen with horror, disbelief.

The stadium lights — flaring. Spurting. Lighting up the darkened sky like the Fourth of July.

1984

Dick Wimmer

୧ଛ

From Baseball Fathers, Baseball Sons

All morning I kept recalling my father and me on those bright, windy Saturdays when I was twelve, journeying up to the Stadium together and across the terrifying catwalks behind his impatient, slope-shouldered stride, "Come on, come on, nothing to be scared of up here," to watch far below the groundskeepers hose down the diamond, the pitchers slowly getting loose, kids scampering along the aisles in pursuit of batting practice homers that bounced high off the silver railings as we eagerly waited for Williams to appear, Raschi meeting with Rizzuto at the mound, the Yankee infield and outfield shifting way around to the right, and Ted, tapping the dirt from his spikes and twisting the bat in his hands, nervously digging into place with that tall, classic stance, our raccoon eyes squinting, and my father smiling and nudging me with a whisper, "This is some game, huh? Glad I took you? Huh? You've got some father. You'll see, just wait'll you have a son of your own."

And now here in California, nearly forty years later, I

have two — a single parent for close to a decade — with the constant link of baseball between us since they could walk, playing and coaching and retelling tales of my boyhood heroes and discovering all their new ones as suddenly, in the wink of an eye, they're both in their teens and the rebellion that's been looming has, in fact, already begun.

But enough of that now, since I have got to get dressed, quickly fitting on my brown baseball cap with the yellow "C" and matching warm-up jacket, then hustling out to my car under a clear blue California sky for the fifteen-minute ride to Calabasas High School. We're halfway through a season of eighteen games in this, my first spring of coaching the JV, and my fourteen-year-old son Geordie, as we take on our archrivals, Agoura, today, while on the adjacent diamond, his older brother, Ceo (pronounced Kee-O), seventeen, will be in center field and batting third for the varsity.

Traffic to my surprise is lighter than usual for a Tuesday afternoon as I breeze along, and my thoughts keep returning once more to Ted Williams and our extraordinary meeting with him almost a year ago last March:

"I can't believe we're really going, Dad, I thought you were just joking when you first talked about it!" Geordie chattered on excitedly as the three of us strapped ourselves aboard the Northwest Orient flight from L.A. to Tampa during spring break and zoomed away across the country, our conversation glittering with the magic names of Boggs and Mattingly, Ozzie and Schmidt, Hershiser and Cal Ripken, Jr. — for those were only a few of the current players we were off to meet and talk to on that once-in-a-lifetime trip, while I reminisced with such stars of my era as Stan the Man Musial, Sandy Koufax, Joe DiMaggio, and my all-time hero, Ted Williams, The Thumper, The Splendid Splinter, Teddy Ballgame, about their fathers and their sons.

At 6:30 the next morning, we were out of our motel and shooting up Route 4 to the lazy little town of Winter Haven, Florida, and Chain O'Lakes Park, home of the Boston Red Sox. There were several diamonds — minor-league fields, we assumed — spread down to the right, and no one on them, as we turned left and headed toward the clubhouse for a prearranged meeting with Ted Williams. I didn't know what to expect: Would he be gruff and acerbic, dismissing me with a rude rebuff as he'd done with so many writers in the past?

We pulled to a stop by the empty press room lounge and ran into Dick Bresciani, the friendly PR man, who was leaving for Fort Myers and a B game against the Royals. He told us that Williams should be here soon, "Nine, nine-thirty, he usually gets in, but you never know, 'cause John Henry, his son's here, too."

Geordie watched in awe as Marty Barrett and Dwight Evans strolled by and then — with a deep breath and a running start — asked for their autographs, and one from the dour Jim Rice (when he was Geordie's age, he'd been a starter for his American Legion team), who strode silently, massively, past, didn't even acknowledge the request until he reached his locker, then turned and muttered, "C'mere," and swiftly scrawled his name. This same Jim Rice, who once hit sixteen consecutive pitches out of Fenway during batting practice, alone before his locker, and my sons and I in the Red Sox clubhouse, no other reporters in sight — for the team had finished 18½ games out the year before (and no one could conceive then of Clemens' Cy Young and the postseason wonders to come) — and no sign of Williams as yet. Only a white golf cart that he alone used. The three of us walking out toward the diamond with the dark green carpet of outfield grass shimmering in the sun, then springy under our feet — surprised how sharply it sloped away from the rim of the infield — as the boys went racing across it, imagining themselves making that great over-the-shoulder, leaping one-hand catch in deep left-center. And my own fantasy that Williams would arrive and ask me to hit, and go crazy at this "Natural's" grace and bat speed as I put out that tall bank of lights, call for McNamara, and "Roy Hobbs" Wimmer will sign a contact right there on the spot!

The sun kept blazing down and still no Williams as, amazingly, we sat alone in the Red Sox dugout and watched Wade Boggs take batting practice. Ceo marveling at his smooth stroke, with more players appearing, starters and rookies we'd never seen, Roger Clemens saying hello, and Geordie detailing Boggs' stats last year ".368, .351 lifetime, only popped out twice —" as he kept lacing line drives into left, center, and right.

At nine-thirty we moved back to the clubhouse with the news that Williams had arrived, was inside, and would be out in a moment. We hurried along, all those boyhood im-ages of my father and me suddenly whirling through my mind.

And there he was! The Splendid Splinter, Teddy Ballgame, the best, no question about it, that I've ever seen — now sixty-seven years old but still Williams as he came urgently striding out, beefy round at the middle and leathery, weather-beaten handsome at an imposing six-four, with his Red Sox cap, sunglasses, white warm-up jacket, sports shirt, and slacks — and was intercepted by me.

"What's this about?" as he continued walking toward the field. "Baseball fathers and baseball sons, Dick Bresciani–" "Well how long'll it take?" "Just a few minutes—" "Awright, well then let's get it over with, don't take too long now." Oh my God, a vision of having just flown three thousand miles for a two-minute interview!

THE SANDLOT GAME

We sat along the right-field line, with the boys before us taking snapshots, and I had to keep blinking and swallowing hard to believe I was finally sitting beside Ted Williams. He'd been my hero so long as I regaled my sons with his prowess that now their love of me had passed through him, whom they'd never seen play, and he'd become their hero, too.

And far from the bristling legend I'd expected, I found a warm and generous man, with great bursts of enthusiasm, quick and bright — who ultimately made me feel as though I were talking to my father (or possibly through my father) in a frozen moment of time.

‏‮‬

Geordie was still staring in awe at the ball Williams had signed and quoting, " 'To Geordie, your pal, Ted Williams.' That's rad, Dad, rad!" when one of the reporters whispered that the tall, dark, and Hollywood handsome boy passing by in a Red Sox uniform with a big blue 9 on the back and wearing two batting gloves was Ted's son, John Henry. I introduced myself and Ceo and Geordie, told him of the project, and we moved into the press room, where the four of us sat alone, Ceo snapping pictures and John Henry shy yet composed.

After, we all headed down to the minor-league fields as John Henry moved into the long, net-enclosed batting cage where his father sat on a bucket behind a small protective screen, former Red Sox first baseman George Scott beside him, and softly tossed up ball after ball to his tall, good-looking son, who took a wide-open, right-handed stance.

"What'd you do that time?" Williams asked, following a swing and a miss, and tossing up another ball.

"I missed it."

Still tossing, "Hips in front of hands."

And John Henry, lean and tense like a high-strung horse now, kept swinging and soon began lining the ball, often as not, off the sides of the cage or over his father's head. And the touching thing to me was how kind, considerate, and understanding Williams was to his son: gentle, prodding, never harsh, always supportive, and backing off when he touched a nerve.

John Henry abruptly asking, "What about my ankle? I keep twisting my ankle when I swing."

"It's OK, it's OK."

"No, it's not OK, that shouldn't be!"

John Henry switching to the left side then as Ted came out of the cage, "He'll see many more right-handers in college," and George Scott began flipping up the balls. Williams standing next to me, both of us wearing our flapping windbreakers, and I thought how hard it was to follow a legend — or rather impossible — to establish who you are. The struggle of all sons? To some degree. To break free and become yourself, realizing as I had over these years that all sons are separate, almost strangers, and should be seen as such, not merely our flesh and blood; and the basic things we can teach them in life are first to walk and then to walk away.

When John Henry was through, I asked if Ceo could follow him in, and unbelievably Williams agreed: John Henry taking over the "pitching" from behind the BP screen as all of us watched, along with a handful of fans and passing minor-leaguers, Ceo in his gray shorts and striped, light blue sports shirt, sneakers and high white socks. But before he began, Williams just had him swing the bat in the cage, no pitching, "Just your normal swing."

And as soon as he did, out came a flurry of rapid comments: "He's hitting down, he's hitting down. Drop your hands, drop your hands. More, more! You're looking at the plate. Look out there, follow the ball. Your hips're going one way and your head another. Hips in front of hands, face the way you wanna hit the ball, hips in front of hands!"

And soon thereafter, left-handed-hitting Ceo began whacking line drives off every part of the cage.

"There! Now he's got it, now he's got it!" Williams whirling around, facing me, and asking, "Where's his head, following the ball, hips in front of hands?"

"Right."

"See, see!"

And for the next thirty minutes, my son hit under the watchful eye of Ted Williams as John Henry kept pitching and Ceo kept ripping shot after shot with that smooth, powerful swing, head down, hips in front of hands, and Williams leaned toward me, "He's a strong kid. How old is he?"

"Sixteen."

"Sixteen? He's good, he's good, just keep that head up and follow the ball."

George Scott asking, "He on a team?"

"Yeah, in Calabasas, California."

Williams leaning toward me again. "And how old is he?"

"Sixteen."

"When'll he be seventeen?"

"August."

"August what?"

"Twenty-fifth."

Williams grinned. "John Henry's on the twenty-sixth!"

Now all the balls were used up as Ceo and John Henry emerged together, Williams and I walking away side by side, and he said, "That'll be a hundred dollars the half hour."

I laughed, "You kidding? You can name your price?"

I asked Geordie if he wanted a turn, but he begged off, shy in the shadow of his brother, afraid to compete, to fail or disappoint. And how much more could I ask of Williams as he hopped in the golfing cart with his son and sped away, at sixty-seven still brimming with life, or rather striding through it, just like he hit, never at rest, twisting impatient hands about the bat. And the three of us wishing we could've seen him swing. But all we were allowed were those rare moments when he'd reveal a stunning flash of that powerful grace that filled me again with wonder and memory of that tall classic stance, nervously digging into place.

1988

Pat Jordan

❧

The Living Legend
From The Suitors of Spring

Stephen Louis Dalkowski, a pitcher, signed a minor-league baseball contract with Kingsport, Tenn., of the Class D Appalachian League shortly after his eighteenth birthday in 1957. He was given his unconditional release by San Jose, Calif., of the Class C California League shortly before his twenty-seventh birthday in 1966. In nine years of professional baseball, mostly in Class D and C towns like Kingsport and San Jose, Pensacola, Fla., and Aberdeen, S.D., Dalkowski won a total of 46 games, lost 80 and fashioned a lifetime 5.67 earned-run average. His best won-lost record was 8-4 with Stockton, Calif., in the California League in 1964. However, throughout much of his career, which covered 11 teams and nine leagues, Dalkowski managed records like 1-9 with an 8.13 ERA at Kingsport; 0-4 with a 12.96 ERA at Pensacola; 7-15 with a 5.14 ERA at Stockton; and 3-12 with an 8.39 ERA at Tri-Cities. Dalkowski never pitched an inning in the major leagues, and pitched only 24 innings as high as Triple A, where his record was 2-3 with a 7.12 ERA.

On May 7, 1966, shortly after his release from baseball, *The Sporting News* carried a blurred, seven-year-old photograph of Dalkowski, along with a brief story headlined LIVING LEGEND RELEASED. The first sentence of that story read as follows: "Steve Dalkowski, a baseball legend in his own time, apparently has thrown his last professional pitch." The story was not considered particularly dramatic at the time since few people even on the periphery of organized baseball had not heard of Steve Dalkowski.

To understand how Dalkowski, a chunky little man with thick glasses and a perpetually dazed expression, became a "legend in his own time," it is necessary to go back 10 years to a hot spring day in Miami, Fla. Dalkowski is pitching batting practice for the Baltimore Orioles while Ted Williams watches curiously from behind the batting cage. After a few minutes Williams picks up a bat and steps into the cage. Reporters and players, who had been watching with only casual interest, move quickly around the cage to watch this classic confrontation. Williams takes three level, disciplined practice swings, cocks his bat and then motions with his head for Dalkowski to deliver the ball. Dalkowski goes into his sparce pump. His right leg rises a few inches off the ground. His left arm pulls back and then flicks out from the side of his body like an attacking cobra. There is a sharp crack as his wrist snaps the ball toward the plate. Then silence. The ball does not rip through the air like most fastballs, but seems to just reappear silently in the catcher's glove as if it had somehow decomposed and then recomposed itself without anyone having followed its progress.

The catcher holds the ball for a few seconds. It is just a few inches under Williams' chin. Williams looks back at the ball, then out a Dalkowski, who is squinting at him. Then he drops his bat and steps out of the cage.

The writers immediately ask Williams how fast Steve Dalkowski really is. Williams, whose eyes were said to be so sharp that he could count the stitches on a baseball as it rotated toward the plate, says that he did not see the pitch, and that Steve Dalkowski is the fastest pitcher he ever faced and probably who ever lived, and that he would be damned if he would ever face him again if he could help it.

Ted Williams was not the only baseball authority who claimed Dalkowski was the fastest pitcher of all time. Paul Richards, Harry Brecheen, Earl Weaver and just about anyone who had ever seen the New Britain, Conn., native throw, claimed he was faster than Feller and Johnson and any of the fabled old-timers. The Orioles, who owned Dalkowski from 1957 to 1965, sent him to the Aberdeen Proving Grounds in 1958 to have Army equipment test the speed of his fastball. The fastest pitcher ever evaluated by such equipment was Bob Feller, whose fastball was clocked at 98.6 mph. On the day Dalkowski threw into the machine, his fastball was clocked at 93.5 mph. But Feller had thrown his fastball from a high mound that added 5 to 8 mph to its speed; Dalkowski had thrown from level ground since there was no mound available. Also, Dalkowski had pitched a game the day before, and that alone would have accounted for at least a 5 to 10 mph loss in speed. And finally, Dalkowski was literally exhausted by the time the machine clocked his fastball because he had to pitch for 40 minutes before he had thrown a fastball within range of the machine's measuring device. All things considered, it was conservatively assumed that Dalkowski's fastball, when right, traveled at well over 105 mph, truly faster than that of anyone who ever lived.

But it was precisely his wildness, almost as much as his speed, that made Dalkowski a "legend in his own time" and eventually prevented him from ever reaching the majors. In nine years of minor-league pitching he walked 1,354 batters in 995 innings. He struck out 1,396. In his last year of high school Dalkowski pitched a no-hitter in which he walked 18 batters and fanned the same number. In 1957 at Kingsport, he led the Appalachian League with 129 walks, 39 wild pitches, and 121 strikeouts in 62 innings. He once walked 21 batters in a Northern League game, and in another contest he struck out 21 batters — both league records. In 1960 Dalkowski set a California League record by granting 262 walks in 170 innings. He fanned the same number. In 1961 he set a Northwest League record of 196 walks in 103 innings while striking out 150 batters.

Stories of Dalkowski's speed and wildness would pass from one minor-league town to another, each player picking them up, embellishing them and passing them on, as if by the mere act of embellishing he was in a sense sharing in those feats. There was the story of the hapless batter whose ear was torn off by a Dalkowski fastball; or the home-plate umpire who was knocked unconscious for 30 minutes by a Dalkowski fastball; or the outfield fence that was splintered by a Dalkowski fastball thrown on a bet; or the brick wall demolished; or the home-plate screen ripped to shreds, scattering all the fans and convincing them to never again sit behind home plate when Steve Dalkowski pitched. And then there was the Williams story. Players who knew of Dalkowski always ended with the Williams story, as if that was the one supreme compliment to his talent.

Inevitably the stories outgrew the man until it was no longer possible to distinguish fact from fiction. But no matter how exaggerated the stories might have become, the fact still remained that Dalkowski struck out and walked more batters per nine-inning game than any other professional pitcher. There was also considerable proof that he was the fastest hurler who ever lived. And it was because of his blinding speed that the Baltimore Orioles put up with him through eight years of little or no success. Every spring the Orioles' management would conduct a new experiment with Dalkowski in an attempt to discipline his talent. They made him throw fastballs at a wooden target. They made him throw on the sidelines until exhausted, under the assumption that once his lively arm was tired and his speed was muted slightly it would be easier for him to throw strikes. They bought him thick Captain Video-type glasses to correct his faulty 20-80, 20-60 vision. They made him pitch batting practice every day for two straight weeks in the hope that facing a batter would help guide his pitches. And finally they made him throw only 15 feet away from his catcher, believing that once he threw strikes from that distance, the distance could be gradually increased to 60 feet, 6 inches, from where he would also throw strikes.

After twenty minutes of throwing at a wooden target the target was in splinters. No matter how long he threw on the sidelines his arm never got tired. His thick glasses only served to further terrify already terrified batters. No matter how long he pitched batting practice he still had trouble throwing the ball inside the cage, let alone over the plate. And after two weeks of throwing at a distance of only 15 feet, Dalkowski could still no more throw a strike from that distance than he could from 60 feet, 6 inches.

In the end, all the experiments failed. There were a number of reasons, not the least of which was the fact that if ever a man was truly possessed by his talent it was Stephen Louis Dalkowski.

"When I signed Steve in 1957," said Baltimore scout Frank McGowan, "he was a shy, introverted kid with absolutely no confidence in himself. Even in high school he was so wild he would walk the ball park. But we gave him a $4000 bonus, which was the limit at the time, because Harry Brecheen said he had the best arm he ever saw. It's possible, too, that Paul Richards might have given Steve a little something under the table because he was no anxious to get hold of him. Everyone knew it was a gamble, he was so wild, but we all thought he was worth it. Now that Steve's out of baseball I feel there were three things in particular that prevented him from making the big leagues. The first was that boy he almost killed in Kingsport. He hit him on the side of the head with a fastball and boy never played ball again. They say he was never quite right in the head after that, either.

"Following that incident Steve was always terrified of hitting somebody. One year Clyde King, his manager at Rochester, put a batter on each side of the plate and made Steve throw to them both simultaneously. He threw five of six strikes right down the middle, possibly because he knew that if he threw the ball either left or right it would hit one of them.

"Another reason he didn't make it was that he was too easily led. He seemed always to be looking for someone to follow, and in the minors he followed the wrong guys. He was never a bad kid, really, but he liked to drink a little, and raise hell at night, which certainly never helped his career. One year I remember we sent him to Pensacola to play under Lou Fitzgerald, an easy-going old-timer. And who do you think Steve got hooked up with down there? Bo Belinski and Steve Barber. That had to be the three fastest, wildest left-handers any manager had to cope with — both on the field and off. Yet I think Steve could have made it if he was ever led by the right guys. Once we put Harry Brecheen behind the mound to talk to him on every pitch. Steve threw nothing but strikes. But the minute Harry walked off, Steve was as wild as ever.

"And finally I think the Orioles made too much of a fuss over Steve in his early years. They were always billing him as the 'fastest pitcher alive,' and I think the publicity hurt him. Stuff like taking him to the Aberdeen Proving Grounds and conducting all those experiments. I think he would have been a lot better off if they had just left him alone in the minors and let him move up by himself... But even that might not have done it, I guess. What it all boiled down to was the fact that Steve never made the major leagues because he never did learn to control Steve Dalkowski — period."

But if he failed to discipline himself and his talent, Dalkowski made a Herculean effort. He never took exception to the many experiments the Orioles' performed with him, even though at times he doubted them. Brecheen once said that if ever a man deserved to make the major leagues it was Dalkowski, "because of the determined way he went at pitching and the cooperation he always showed in those long hours of work."

Many people close to Dalkowski felt he suffered those experiments too good-naturedly, that he should have gotten angry and rebelled against them. But rather than become angry with all the interest in him, he seemed bewildered and confused by it. No matter how many hours he worked in the distant bullpens of Aberdeen and Kingsport and Pensacola, Dalkowski never really seemed a part of the experiments. He always gave the impression that he viewed them from outside himself, as if they were being conducted not on him personally but on a body that belonged only partly to him and partly to a lot of other people who had a stake in him.

Furthermore, people said, he never got angry enough for

success. If he could only begrudge someone else their success, if he could only become mad at those with inferior talent who surpassed him, it might inspire him to succeed. But he said he never envied anyone else's success, and then added, "I never met a ballplayer I didn't like."

"No one ever wanted to succeed more than Steve," said Ken Cullum, a friend of Dalkowski's from New Britain. "He would run through a brick wall if he had to. But he always seemed afraid that his success would have to come at the expense of someone else. And he could never hurt anyone like that."

By 1962 the Orioles had tired of Dalkowski. The previous year they had come up with four young pitchers, Steve Barber, Chuck Estrada, Milt Pappas, and Jack Fisher, who together had won 56 games, and now they no longer worried about Dalkowski's progress. He was shipped to Elmira of the Class A Eastern League, and immediately the front office began scanning their lower minor-league rosters to see where they could ship him next once he became insufferable to manager Earl Weaver. But under Weaver, an intense, roly-poly little man, Dalkowski began to throw strikes — relatively speaking. For the first time in his career he walked fewer batters (114) than innings pitched (160), while still striking out a substantial number (192). He won 7 games, lost 10, and posted a respectable 3.04 ERA. He led the league in shutouts with 6, and he also completed 8 of 19 starts, the most of his career. The following spring with the Orioles at Miami, Dalkowski said Earl Weaver had given him confidence.

"I felt that Steve had been given every tip on control that was ever known," said Weaver. "I knew that the smartest pitching coaches in baseball had worked with him. There wasn't anything I could tell him that he hadn't heard a hundred times before. The one thing I did try to do was keep quiet."

During the spring of 1963 Dalkowski's progress was the talk of the Orioles' training camp. In a two-inning relief stint against the Dodgers he fanned five and gave up no hits or walks. Harry Brecheen said that Dalkowski was just the short reliever the Orioles had been looking for, and then added: "The boy has come a long way. There is no doubt of his improvement. He is more settled as an individual and he deserves to make it. Steve is a good kid."

Toward the end of spring training Dalkowski was interviewed by a reporter who asked him if all the strenuous activity he had placed on his arm had ever damaged it through the years. Dalkowski admitted that he had lost a little off his fastball at the age of 23, but then said, no, he had never really had a sore arm in his life. A few days later in an exhibition game, Dalkowski fielded a bunt and threw off-balance to first base. He got the runner, but also pinched a muscle in his elbow. He was never the same pitcher again.

The Orioles shipped him to Rochester of the International League, hoping that his arm might come around. But he pitched only 12 innings there, then 29 innings at Elmira. For the first time in his career he was unable to average one strikeout per inning. The following season he started at Elmira and then drifted down to Stockton, where he was 8-4 with a 2.83 ERA. His arm apparently had begun to heal, but he hurt it again in 1965 and was sent to Tri-Cities of the Class B Northwest League. In 1961 he had fanned 150 batters in 103 innings at Tri-Cities; in 1965 he managed only 62 strikeouts in 84 innings, the worst record of his career. In midseason the Orioles released him, and he was picked up by the Los Angeles Angels and sent to San Jose. The following spring the Angels gave him his unconditional release.

Today, five years after he left baseball, Dalkowski's name still evokes recognition from anyone who ever participated in professional baseball. Recently Dick Schaap, the noted sportswriter, asked Tom Seaver to name the fastest pitcher ever. Seaver did not hesitate in answering "Steve Dalkowski," although he added he had never seen him pitch.

But Steve Dalkowski's real fame rests not with the Tom Seavers in cities such as New York. Instead, it lies in all those low minor-league towns like Wellsville and Leesburg and Yakima and Stockton, or wherever talented but erratic young players are struggling toward the major leagues. To these minor-leaguers Dalkowski will always symbolize every frustration and elation they have ever felt because of their God-given talent. They take pride in recalling his successes, as if his was the ultimate talent, and his struggle to discipline it, the ultimate struggle. If Steve Dalkowski had succeeded it would have given proof to their own future success. But even his failure does not diminish him, for it was not the result of deficiency but of excess. He was too fast. His ball moved too much. His talent was superhuman. To young players he is proof that failure is not always due to a dearth of physical talent. So, in a way, Dalkowski's lack of achievement softens the possibility of their own imminent failures.

Dalkowski could only have succeeded if he had tempered his blazing speed with control and discipline — in short, had compromised his fastball, because with control inevitably comes loss of speed. His wildness can be considered a refusal to give up any of his speed, even in the hope of gaining control and big-league glory. Instead, Dalkowski settled for those isolated, pure, distilled moments of private success attributable solely to talent. And those moments could never be dimmed, because their purity was inherent in his talent. That he never won a major league game, never became a star, is not important to young ballplayers who hold him in such reverence. All that matters is that once, just once, Steve Dalkowski threw a fastball so hard that Ted Williams never even saw it. No one else can claim that.

1973

 ಶ

Note: In 1995, Pat Jordan again wrote about Dalkowski

Everyone has theory as to why Steve never made the majors. Some people called it fate — the sore arm — which helped embellish his legend. Others said it was because he drank too much — that's why he was wild. He drank and was wild because of that batter he almost killed in Kingsport.

I thought there was a bit of truth in all of these theories until I tracked him down in the early '80s in Bakersfield, Calif. He had just been released, again, from the rehab center for alcoholism. He told me to come to his trailer-camp apartment at 4 a.m. He met me at the door, a funny-looking, little man squinting at me through thick eyeglasses. He didn't look like the fastest pitcher who ever lived, or, for that matter, an athlete. He had skinny arms and a little paunch. A timid little man, who reminded me of Mr. Peepers from the '50s TV show.

We talked in his living room for a while about why he never made the majors. He was rational, at first, but after a few trips to the bathroom, he began to slur his words. I learned later that he kept a bottle of wine in the bathroom and sipped it from the moment he woke. That's why he wanted me there at 4 a.m., before he got drunk and had to go off to work at 6 a.m.

He stood in the middle of the room, wobbly, and tried to show me his pitching motion. He pumped, reared back unsteadily, and delivered. It was a funny, short-armed motion, his arm flipping out from the side of his body like an attacking snake. There was nothing classic about it, no big league kick, nothing, just the motion of a man who never really would have been a pitcher if not for his God-given gift, which he could never understand.

He was just an ordinary man, not an athlete, who was given a gift he had no idea what to do with. It was as if he was outside himself looking at his arm fling those fastballs, and he was just as amazed as everyone else.

"Why didn't I make it?" Dalkowski said. "I don't know. I could never get it right." He was as confused by it as everyone else. He would have been so much happier, I thought then, if he had just worked in a factory. His gift turned into a curse.

At 6 a.m. Steve asked me to drive him to work. I drove him through the dark, foggy back streets of Bakersfield until we came to the Mexican section of town. Steve got out and stood in the shadows by a liquor store with a blinking, neon tequila sign. Other men joined him. Like Steve, they had paper bags they were drinking from. Then a flat bed truck pulled up and the men jumped in. I followed the truck out of town to a vast field of vegetables. Steve was a migrant farm worker.

"I'm the fastest potato picker," he said. His secret? He put one bottle of wine at one end of a row, and another bottle a the other, and then picked furiously from bottle to bottle.

The truck dropped off one man at a time, then drove a few hundred yards and dropped off another man. When I saw Steve jump off the truck, I pulled over to the side of the road and watched. He got down on his knees in the gray, damp, foggy, early morning and began to pick potatoes up the row. He grew smaller as he picked, until, at the far end, he was only a tiny, dark figure, on his knees, the fastest pitcher who ever lived.

❧

Numerous attempts to find Steve Dalkowski were in vain.
His path was traced from Bakersfield to Oklahoma City, Okla.,
his last known address as of January 1994.

Steven Louis Dalkowski

Born June 3, 1939 at New Britain, CT.
Threw left. Batted left. Height: 5-10. Weight: 170.
One of fastest and widest pitchers in minor league history.

YEAR	CLUB	LEAGUE	G	IP	W	L	H	R	ER	BB	SO	ERA
1957	Kingsport	Appalachian	15	62	1	8	22	68	56	129	121	8.13
1958	Knoxville	SALLY	11	42	1	4	17	41	39	95	82	7.93
	Wilson	Carolina	8	14	0	1	7	19	19	38	29	12.21
	Aberdeen	Northern	11	62	3	5	29	50	44	112	121	6.39
1959	Aberdeen	Northern	12	59	4	3	30	43	37	110	99	5.64
	Pensacola	Alabama-Florida	7	25	0	4	11	38	36	80	43	12.96
1960	Stockton	California	32	170	7	15	105	120	97	262	262	5.14
1961	Kennewick	Northwest	31	103	3	12	75	117	96	196	150	8.39
1962	Elmira	Eastern	31	160	7	10	117	61	54	114	192	3.04
1963	Elmira	Eastern	13	29	2	2	20	10	9	26	28	2.79
	Rochester	International	12	12	0	2	7	8	8	14	8	6.00
1964	Elmira	Eastern	8	15	0	1	17	12	10	19	16	6.00
	Stockton	California	20	108	8	4	91	40	34	62	141	2.83
	Columbus	International	3	12	2	1	15	11	11	11	9	8.25
1965	Kennewick	Northwest	16	84	6	5	84	60	48	52	62	5.14
	San Jose	California	6	38	2	3	35	25	20	34	33	4.74
		Minor	236	995	46	80	682	723	618	1354	1396	5.59

Jim Murray

ﾞ&

Koufax the King
From The Sporting World
of Jim Murray

Sandy Koufax belongs in baseball about the way Albert Schweitzer belongs in a twist joint. After midnight.

You get the feeling when you see him in the monkey suit that someone is going to change the gender of that old bromide and demand, "What's a nice young fellow like you doing in a place like this? Now, get out of those sweat clothes and into medical school."

In a game historically dominated by extroverted young roughnecks from the oil fields or the cotton patches, Sandy comes from a nice Jewish family in Brooklyn. Scholarship and good manners were revered. He has never worn a pair of overalls in his life. He had the kind of childhood where someone probably cried when he got his first haircut.

He is shy, considerate. He prefers his music great, not loud. On plane trips, he plays word games with the press, not Hearts with the boys. There are many intelligent, well-educated boys in baseball today, many of them on the Dodgers, but almost every major-league ballplayer has violence somewhere within him. They are a throwback to a long line of warriors. Sandy, on the other hand, seems a captive of baseball, trapped by his talent, not his instincts.

You never see him in the bars. The Baseball Annies, forlorn, adoring little creatures who jump in elevators with the single boys on road trips and hang around lobbies in their best dresses and perfume and wobbly high heels, look at Sandy longingly as he hurries by after a game, as if they'd like to take him home and chain him there. But Sandy ignores them. His tastes do not run to grown-up autograph hounds. He wants a wife, not a fan. It's going to be difficult to find her now.

The plain truth is Sandy might not even follow baseball if he weren't in it. He is probably the only guy in the league who not only understands what is going on in Vietnam but cares. The team is proud of him and he is popular — but in a special way that a brother who went away to become a lawyer is looked up to by the family in which not everybody could make it.

He is baseball's pampered child, but it has never given him a day's temperament. They never let him ride the leaky buses or play in ballparks so dim you couldn't even play cards. Sandy never spent an hour in the minor leagues. You don't send a Rembrandt around to drug store galleries to languish among all those prints of pooped Indians slumped over dying horses. They wanted Sandy right where they could see him, not out playing in traffic with all those ruffians where he might get hurt.

Anyone who ever watched him pitch could understand why. Only a handful of men in history could put the spin and velocity on a thrown ball that he did or have the wildness. Sandy never threw at hitters. But sometimes it would have been better if he did. Where Sandy was aiming the ball was the safest place to be.

But the Dodgers were as patient with him as a poor family with a relative with lots of money and a bad heart. The only suspense was whether Sandy would care enough for the game. There was always a lurking suspicion that, once he took the bonus money, the attitude was "Baseball, Schmaseball, as long as you got the money." But this was the opinion of the know-it-alls who didn't know Sandy. Sandy had a strong sense of duty and even when the duty lay with the odd little world of baseball, Sandy discharged it.

Gradually, almost imperceptibly, Sandy became a pitcher instead of a refugee from a white collar. He began to pitch victoriously instead of brilliantly. He pitched two no-hit games. In baseball, one can be a freak. Two establishes a trend.

Pitchers are one-purpose human beings. But in Sandy's case, it's ridiculous. He can field a thrown ball like a guy groping for a towel with soap in his eyes. He could run faster on snowshoes. On a team that beats out infield hits, he has trouble beating out outfield hits. He hit one to Frank Robinson in right field in the Coliseum and by the time he turned around to the umpire to say, "What do you do next?," it was a routine out from the right fielder to the first baseman. They have to drop paper to show him the way from first to third. He got a home run off Warren Spahn one night and they say they had to pull Spahnie down off a hotel ledge later.

They rub Sandy down for hours the day before he pitches. They'd probably get him a butler and a footman if he held out for them. He is the Dodger' Man With the Golden Arm.

But being a great pitcher does not always add up to being a good one. Despite his glittering career and statistics that glow in the dark, Sandy had never won a BIG game. Sometimes, an invisible gremlin of fear plucks at the sleeves of the best of them when the stakes are high and the hour is late and there are no second chances. The league had long since discarded the canard, "with Koufax, stay close to him and you beat him." But no one was ready to bluster that Sandy would run neck-and-neck with the cool-heads like Hubbell and Ford. With 30,000 people screaming at him to drop the brush, even Rembrandt might come out with a picture of a pooped Indian.

The pressure on Sandy Tuesday was about what it is at 40 fathoms without a snorkel. It was a baseball Battle of the Marne with reporters from all over the league looking up synonyms for the word "choke" and trying to think of ways to shorten "collapse" for headline purposes. It was a night for throwing hysterical curves that bounce, for shooting fast balls over the backstop, for ending up the night kicking the locker and drying your eyes instead of starring on the pastgame show.

Sandy Koufax threw 87 pitches. Fifty seven of them were fastballs and 47 of these were strikes. He threw 30 curves and 20 of them were strikes. The St. Louis Cardinal "attack" up to the 7th inning consisted of one hit batsman and an errored (by Koufax) bunt. With men on second and third and only one out, it was a time to listen closely for the hiss of gas. Koufax reared back and the next two hitters just aimed the bat where they thought they heard the ball go by. One of them managed to hit it all the way back to the pitcher's mound. Sandy trapped it as deftly as a guy chasing soap around the bottom of the bathtub but it was so tame, not even he could misplay it. That, it so happens, was the old ball game.

Sandy Koufax stood calmly in the locker room later explaining patiently how it had been a routine night. There was no suggestion that this night he had become a professional pitcher and that the prophets who sneered at him as Little Lord Fauntleroy with a cannon for an arm could now claim, "I knew it all the time." And Mrs. Koufax, who lost an architect in the family, could now say she had gained a star.

1961

Peter Gammons

ᘒ

The Throes of Tossing a Baseball
From The Boston Globe

Dave Engle was hitting fungoes as a coach for the Tucson Toros last week when a young catcher from another team asked to talk to him privately. "The kid knew I had the problem," says Engle. "He didn't think anyone really knew about it yet, so he needed to talk. He's desperately trying to find out what to do before people notice. It gets around and he goes haywire and a private hell becomes public."

Engle knows about going haywire. He is thirty-five and could still be catching and making millions. Instead, he is a $20,000-a-year coach in Tucson because he couldn't throw a baseball back to the pitcher.

"What's more natural than playing catch?" Engle says. "Yeah, well, nothing's tougher when you go haywire."

It happened to Steve Blass, who less than two years after being the World Series MVP couldn't pitch to a batter. Joe Cowley similarly went from a twelve-game winner with the Yankees in 1986 to not being able to come within two feet of the plate. In March 1979, the Red Sox's two best prospects, Bobby Sprowl and Steve Schneck, threw pitches up onto screens and hit batters in the on-deck circle. Steve Sax once could not pick up a ball and throw it seventy-five feet from his position at second base to the first baseman. Anyone who has watched Mets catcher Mackey Sasser the last couple of years has seen his throwing problems. Intentional walks and throwing to bases have become serious problems for Matt Young after two years of obscurity and one year in front of no one in Seattle. Darrell Johnson was out of baseball for a year because of it. Jerry Moses almost had to give it up. Mets catcher Phil Lombardi had to quit. "That was my boyhood dream," Lombardi told the New York *Times*, "and I was going to the park feeling sick to my stomach."

Harvey Dorfman, a psychologist — and former coach, counselor and teacher — who works with the Oakland Athletics, is a lighthouse for any troubled player from any organization and has co-authored (with Karl Kuehl) *The Mental Game of Baseball*. He has talked to thousands of players. One, a 98-mph throwing kid named Steve Gasser, couldn't hit the wall of Dorfman's house in Prescott, Arizona.

"These problems almost always can be traced to some trauma," says Dorfman. "Ray Fosse had the problem. He couldn't throw the ball to the pitcher. A couple of years ago we started talking, and he traced it back to its inception. He was a rookie. Luis Tiant was the ace of the Cleveland staff. Ray made a couple of throws that were off. Tiant stuck his glove in front of his face and said, 'Throw the ball here, [expletive].' Ray related how it became imperative to hit Tiant's glove. He told himself, I have to do this. It becomes a life-threatening situation; breathing stops and the brain makes it so, physiologically, you can't throw the ball.

"But it all goes back to trauma, and traumatic memory forces one to replicate the experience. Put a board three feet wide down in your living room and you can walk down it fine. Put it across the Grand Canyon and feel your legs. Well, to Ray Fosse or Steve Gasser, Steve Blass or Bobby Sprowl, they feel as if they're falling into the Grand Canyon on every throw.

"The more you think about it, the worse it becomes, and negative advice continually makes things worse. I know a pitcher who has the problem who constantly wakes up from a dream where he has thrown a ball in the bullpen that is wild, gets out on the field and the game is stopped while the ball is retrieved and everyone looks at him. He wakes up with this dream every night."

ε♥

Bobby Sprowl doesn't remember how many innings or how many runs he allowed that March afternoon in 1979 in Daytona Beach. "I guess I've tried to block some of that out," Sprowl says. "But I remember the pitch that hit the tarp two thirds of the way up to the press box. And that I never should have gone out there."

Sprowl, now the pitching coach at his alma mater, the University of Alabama, claims he doesn't believe it was the trauma of being thrown into the Red Sox's collapse and the Boston Massacre that caused him to go haywire. But he does come under Dorfman's category of being rushed with unrealistic expectations. Sprowl was supposed to be the phenom savior, thrust into the fray against Joe Morgan's recommendation. After a decent start in which he lost, 4-1, to Jim Palmer in Baltimore, Sprowl was asked to stop a Yankee sweep on September 10; he never made it out of the first inning. "I didn't pitch that badly, I wasn't really wild," Sprowl says.

But the first time he threw batting practice the next spring, he began to have problems throwing strikes. Three veteran players became angry. Rick Burleson flung down his bat and walked out. Another whom Sprowl refuses to identify yelled to a coach, "Get this [expletive] minor-leaguer out of here. This is supposed to be the big leagues and this [expletive] is going to kill someone." Reminded that Sprowl indeed had pitched in the big leagues in September, the player said, "That was big-league pitching?"

Sprowl was a nervous sort who fidgeted with his hands, contrary to minor-league coach Johnny Podres' report to Don Zimmer that Sprowl "has ice water in his veins." He lacked social self-confidence and, as his room at the Holiday Inn was next to this reporter's, often came next door to chat at night. "I don't understand what's happening," he said one night. "It's embarrassing, and players act as if I'm embarrassing them."

Sprowl recalls that it kept unraveling. "I couldn't throw the ball to a catcher, I couldn't breathe properly," he says. "Guys were telling me that I was gripping the ball too tight. Everyone had a different idea. I remember trying to throw to a target I drew on a wall; I not only hit the target, but I could have thrown it through the wall. But put a catcher and a hitter out there . . .

"When I started taking abuse from teammates, it got more and more frustrating. At first I tried telling hitters I was just missing, but they wouldn't listen. Oh well, at least I got back to the big leagues. I wasn't hopeless. I know this: I watch Mackey Sasser on TV and I feel for him. God, I feel for him."

After going all the way back to Winter Haven, Florida, Sprowl was included in the deal for Bob Watson and eventually appeared in nineteen games for the Astros from 1979-81. He never won a game.

"After that spring, he never threw the ball as hard and had the great slider he had in the minors," says Bruce Hurst, who after successful work with Dorfman in 1983 tried to get

Sprowl to talk to him. "Bobby Sprowl was awesome before he went haywire. But after that, he never threw the ball with abandon again. People ask me who was the best of our little lefty group — John Tudor, Bobby Ojeda or me. I tell them, 'Bobby Sprowl was the best left-hander the Red Sox developed since Mel Parnell.' But just as he was close to being developed, the wires got crossed."

Says Sprowl, "Kevin Saucier scouts this area, so I see him a lot. The same thing happened to him. We talk about what happened, but neither of us really knows. Every once in a while I'll be throwing batting practice, and I start thinking in the back of my mind what happened. But I'm O.K. I love what I'm doing.

"When I was coaching junior college, I had a kid who developed this problem. I talked to him about my problem and told him to just go to the bullpen and throw and throw and throw until it became natural again. He overcame it and is in the minors. I had another kid this year at 'Bama that the Yankees drafted; I don't think he will overcome it. I try to help."

"It's hard for Sprowl to help because he never identified the cause of his problem," says Dorfman. "He's thirty-five right now. He'd probably still be in the big leagues."

&

Sprowl was not alone that spring of 1979. The best young pitcher in the Red Sox organization was Schneck, a twenty-three-year old right-hander who was the Double A pitcher of the year with a 15-7, 2.15 record; his 2½-season minor-league ERA was 2.13.

"I had put tremendous pressure on myself, as I'd believed my press clippings about making the club," says Schneck. "I went to Puerto Rico near the end of the winter season to be completely ready to make the team, and right at the end I had some problems with feeling at the tips of my fingers."

Was it psychosomatic?

"I don't know," he says. "It all happened so fast. Everything went haywire, and I had no feeling in my fingertips. But I don't know which came first."

Schneck's fastball skittered and ran in and out of the strike zone. Spring training 1979 started out harmless enough. "I was having trouble throwing the ball over the plate and had some trouble with the feeling, but I wasn't awful or anything," he says. "I had some trouble throwing strikes a couple of times in BP, and some veterans started yelling at me. It crushed me. I mean, here I was a kid, nervous, with all sorts of expectations and pressures, and I felt humiliated.

"Right before the games were to start, I was throwing in the bullpen and having trouble hitting Bob Montgomery's glove. He finally said 'Kid, I'm not going to move. If you can't throw it over the plate here, I'm going to let it go.' As Zimmer, Al Jackson, writers and fans watched, the balls kept rolling away. Then when I warmed up for my first appearance against the Tigers, the same thing happened. Montgomery kept letting the balls go by him. Only this time there were six thousand people in the stands, and I felt as if every one of them was watching me. It was the worst experience of my life, and I remember it as if it were twenty minutes ago." All Monty was trying to do was help Schneck concentrate, but ...

"A week later, they had me warming up on the left mound in the two-mound bullpen in Winter Haven," recalls Schneck. "The pitcher on the right mound — Joel Finch, I think — had a batter in the right-handed batter's box. I hit the guy in the head."

Three weeks after that, Schneck was sent down to work with the kids who hadn't made the Winter Haven or Winston-Salem rosters and would play in the extended spring program until June. He started against Harvard, and after walking the first six hitters, he wound up for the first pitch to the seventh hitter. He hit the batter in the on-deck circle and left the mound.

"I tried throwing with my eyes closed, and I threw strikes O.K." says Schneck. "During the extended spring, Eddie Popowski and Rac Slider did everything they could to restore my self-confidence and esteem, but when I got to Pawtucket, I was never the same." He was 8-13 with a 4.67 ERA and led the league with 101 walks in 143 innings. "The next spring, I was throwing balls up on backstops, and I told Ed Kenney I didn't know if I could go through it again." He tried a comeback in the Detroit system but had the same problem and retired.

Schneck now works with former Pawtucket outfielder Barry Butera running a baseball school in New Orleans. One of their pupils was Will Clark, who works out with them occasionally in the winter. "Schneck has as good stuff as anyone in the National League," says Clark.

Schneck, who has a bunch of no-hitters for Triple-A Sporting Goods in a semipro league, talked to Hurst about coming back and thought about a tryout with the Mets but changed his mind.

"I don't know if I could do it in front of crowds now," says Schneck. "One part of me wants to try it again, but the other part recalls what I went through. Some things you can't erase from one's memory."

❧

Blass would prefer that he not have a disease named after him. He is a broadcaster with the Pirates now, an outgoing, insightful, gregarious man who also prefers not to talk about what he went through. He is remembered for Steve Blass disease more than his extraordinary pitching, which included eighty-one wins over five years, including a 2-0 shutout in the seventh game of the 1971 World Series. After that Series, he was 19-8. And after that, his record reads:

| 1973 Pittsburgh | 3-9 9.81 ERA | 84 BB 27 K |
| 1974 Charleston | 2-8 9.74 ERA | 103 BB 26 K |

"He was a little wild in spring training in 1973, but no one noticed," says Pirate coach Milt May, who caught Blass' first two starts that year. "He walked five or six in his first start. Nothing I noticed. Then in his next outing, he was facing the Braves. He went 3-and-0 on Ralph Garr leading off, and the fourth ball was behind him. Then three more fastballs, way out of the strike zone, to Marty Perez. I called for a slider. He threw it behind Perez. Then I knew something was haywire.

"It got worse and worse. But you know what's weird? Warming up in the bullpen, he always had his same great stuff, right on the black. Put a batter up there, and he couldn't throw it close."

John Curtis still recalls the day Blass threw a pitch that landed in the stands halfway between third and home in a spring training game in 1974 in which Blass walked the first eight batters.

Blass told Roger Angell — who retold Blass' tale in the unforgettable piece "Gone for Good" (republished this spring in Angell's *Once More Around the Ballpark*) — that he doesn't to this day know what happened. But he vividly recalled the spring of 1974: "We have a custom in the early spring that calls for pitchers to throw five minutes of batting practice every day. Well, the day before the first workout, I woke up at 4:30 in the morning. I was so worried that I couldn't get back to sleep — and this was just throwing to pitchers. I don't remember what happened that first time, but I know that I was tense and anxious every time I went out."

Angell quoted former Pirate pitcher and broadcaster Nellie King: "I think there's a lost kid in Steve. I remember after the 1971 World Series he said, 'I didn't think I was as good as this.' He seemed truly surprised at what he'd done. The child in him is such a great thing, and maybe suddenly he was afraid he was losing it. It was being forced out of him. Being good up here is so tough — people have no idea. It gets much worse when you have to repeat it: 'We know you're great. Do it again for me.' Pretty soon you're trying so hard, you can't function."

༈

Dorfman brings up Dale Murphy. Now, Murphy has been a great player, but he was legend. There was the spring training game when he was catching and tried to throw to second, and center fielder Barry Bonnell caught it on the fly. Or the time he hit his pitcher in the derriere in Richmond.

"It was so bad that he couldn't throw the ball to the third baseman after a strikeout," says Pirate coach Gene Lamont. "He'd wind up, and the left fielder would race over behind the third baseman, catch the ball and relay it to the shortstop."

"Murphy had the pressures of being the future of the entire Braves franchise," says Dorfman, who has spent countless hours with Murphy, baseball's ultimate gentleman. "He finally had to get to a position where he could throw. He went from catcher to first and finally relaxed in the outfield. I've worked with Brad Komminsk, who underwent a similar buildup and pressure later. I'll guarantee you some of those buildups Sparky Anderson has laid on people has hurt some." One very nice person named Chris Pittaro was ruined by being Sparky's "best rookie I've ever seen" when he moved Lou Whitaker to third base for forty-eight hours.

"Some players are bothered by having to repeat success,"

says Dorfman. For instance, when Sonny Siebert won his seventeenth game the first week of September 1971, he didn't want to pitch the rest of the way, saying, "If I win twenty, they'll expect me to do it again." Dorfman says, "That isn't as uncommon as you'd think. I've worked with one former major-league pitcher who says that every time he won, he'd go get drunk, wasted. If he lost, it was normal." Bruce Swango got $100,000 in the early 1950s and couldn't pitch in front of crowds.

"There's nothing funny about any of these problems," says Dorfman. "These are human beings with human conditions."

&

In March 1985, Engle was twenty-eight years old and a pretty good player on the rising Minnesota Twins. He'd batted .305 and .266 the previous two seasons while converting from the outfield to catcher. He'd made the 1984 All-Star team. He had grown up with baseball, as his father not only was Ted Williams' high school catcher but also ran the Ted Williams Camp in Lakeville; father and son drove cross-country from San Diego every June to Lakeville. "Baseball was my life," says the Tucson coach.

"I was catching batting practice and threw a ball back to the pitcher — normally," says Engle. "But it ticked the top of the screen in front of the pitcher and broke his nose. After that, I started occasionally flipping the ball — high in the air, so it came down like a parachute over the screen. Only I started doing it more and more, and before I knew it, I was throwing that way.

"One day Billy Gardner forced me to come out and make hundreds of throws; I threw thirty or forty balls into center field, I felt humiliated, and it got worse. Calvin Griffith called me into his office and aired me out, saying that I was making the pitchers work too hard catching my throws and it was costing them velocity and strength at the end of games. The great thing was that I played for one of the great teams of all time, and my teammates — especially Tom Brunansky, Gary Gaetti and Kent Hrbek — did everything they could to help me. At first, sure, they made fun of me; but as soon as they realized that it was serious, they rallied behind and beside me.

"It started to get worse as the season went along, and I think the day it all went haywire was against Oakland. I lobbed the ball back to the mound, and Alfredo Griffin stole third. That was the beginning of a nightmare. It got so I felt as if I were climbing up a rock on a mountain, and when I approached the top there was a rattlesnake. Every throw became life-threatening.

"It still haunts me, too. I dream about it. I wake up at night thinking about it. Every once in a while I'll be catching someone in BP and it'll come back. Or I'll be throwing BP and I have trouble. I figure it cost me a minimum of five million dollars, maybe more, when I see Rick Cerone and Jamie Quirk still catching."

The Twins unloaded him after the 1985 season, and he bounced from Detroit to Nashville to Montreal to Milwaukee and finally, last year, Oklahoma City.

"I still enjoy the game, and I love working with these kids," Engle says. "But I hope I get over this sometime. I hope I can sleep right again."

❧

In 1988, the Dodgers had the fifth pick in the country and selected a right-handed pitcher from Cal State, Los Angeles, named Bill Bene. The following year, Bene — who'd always had wildness problems — went off the deep end. They tried to use him in an extended spring simulated game; he hit the first batter and broke his hand. Then they tried having him throw with an inflatable doll in the batter's box.

"That got reported and all it did was publicly humiliate the poor kid," says Dorfman. Bene's 1989-90 record in Vero Beach, Bakersfield and Salem: 1-14, 8.86 ERA, 152 walks, 83 innings. One night last summer he threw five straight pitches off the backstop.

Sasser, who works with Dr. Allan Lans, the Mets' psychologist, goes through a series of bizarre motions trying to throw the ball back to the mound. He double-pumps, then leans back. Tim McCarver says many umpires try to help him by letting him lean back on them, but the arc of his throws has resulted in stolen bases and humiliation. Broadcaster Fran Healy relates to Sasser, because he went through the same thing in Kansas City.

"Throwing the ball back to the pitcher is not the real problem," says Lans. "The real problem may have a multitude of causes." Some are complex, involving fear of failure or parental expectation. Some involve other expectations, and can be traced — like Fosse's — right to the field.

Steve Sax understands how the night can torment a player with this problem. "I'd wake up in the night sweating, worried, thinking about the problem," says the second baseman. "I remember Tommy Lasorda screaming at me: 'You can hit .290. How many big-leaguers can do that? You can steal forty bases. How many big-leaguers can do that? *But do you know how many millions of broads can play catch — and you can't?'* But he hadn't been through this."

Right out of Dorfman's book, Sax can trace his famous throwing problems back to a traumatic experience in 1983. "We were playing a game against Montreal in April, and I took a relay in the outfield," Sax recalls. "The runner stopped at third, but I stupidly whirled and threw to the plate. The ball bounced past the catcher, and the run scored. It cost us the game. That got it started. All of a sudden, I was afraid to throw. I don't know what it was. I know I had put a lot of pressure on myself with the buildup as the next great Dodger player, the future batting champion and stuff like that. But by the All-Star break I had twenty-six errors and never slept. I was in a snowball rolling through hell.

"They tried to tell me it was a mechanical thing; of course, it wasn't. I just decided to go out there every day and try to work on it until my proper throwing became motor-mechanical again. I'd take a sanitary (stocking], tie it across my face and throw blindfolded. I worked it out. One thing: it never affected me on double play balls where I had no time to think, and eventually I overcame it. Now, I want the ball hit to me. But I wouldn't wish that problem on anyone. And I'm sure the causes are different in every case."

Sax deserves to be remembered not for having the problem but for working it out. "Some guys disguise it," says Sax. "I didn't want to. I wanted it addressed."

Steve Garvey was one who successfully disguised his throwing phobia. But in the 1974 World Series, the A's knew he would never field a bunt and throw to another base, so every time someone was on base, they bunted to Garvey. Part of that was Los Angeles. If Garvey hadn't been able to throw in Boston, New York or Philadelphia . . .

ह৯

Dorfman refuses to discuss Matt Young's problems, "because I worked with him." All he will say is, "Matt had one very bad incident in L.A.," that "Matt's a very sad story" and "You'll never know how much the pressure of the contract eats at him. That's a tough thing to live with." In fact, in spring training, it so bothered San Francisco's Bud Black that he sat down with Dorfman to talk out the pressures of his expectations. "Remember, the guys most affected are usually responsible, good and intelligent," says Dorfman. "Most feel the more they talk, the more people notice."

Young had throwing problems when he signed with the Mariners. "I used to tell him not to throw to first base on a ground ball, and never to pick anyone off," says A's scout Jeff Scott, Young's rookie league manager. But somewhere along the line, it became a mental thing. Last year, he made three times as many errors as Cal Ripken and hit two first-base coaches. He couldn't give intentional walks normally.

Early in the season, Young had few chances and usually grabbed a ground ball and sprinted toward first. But then came an intentional walk that went haywire. One night he threw several warm-up pitches against the screen. Then came a couple of wild throws ...

It astounds baseball people that the Red Sox apparently knew nothing of Young's problems when they committed $6.35 million to him, especially in the home of the leather-lungs, where every game is a life-or-death matter.

But it isn't funny, because if Young didn't care, he wouldn't have the problem. It wasn't funny when it happened to Joe Sparma in the late 1960s, starting as an inability to throw to bases and ending up, as Jim Leyland remembers, "with a pitch off a lightpole." Or when a great Texas pitching prospect named Jim Gideon couldn't warm up. Or when veteran catcher Johnny Edwards had to carry the ball to the pitcher. Or when Dick Radatz threw twenty-one straight balls in an exhibition game.

"Maybe the best way to be is to believe ignorance is bliss," says Dorfman. "Maybe it's best not to feel responsibility, to not care or be smart enough so even traumatic memory can take effect." Maybe it's best to have what Philip Roth called "infantryman's heart." Or what John Keegan called "the face of battle." That is, the most common parts of heroism from medieval wars to Vietnam were drugs and alcohol that prevented men from going haywire.

For many, the trait that makes a man heroic and an athlete victorious is what you would not want in your son. Would Dave Engle and Bobby Sprowl sell their souls — that which makes them human — to be rich and great and famous?

1991

John Hough, Jr.

ₔ

From A Player for a Moment

Robin Roberts, meanwhile, decided to try to pitch his way to the big leagues the hard way. The Phillies, perhaps for sentimental reasons, agreed to let him join their double-A team in Reading, Pennsylvania. One of the Phillies' radio announcers was Richie Ashburn, a former Phillies teammate of Roberts'. Ashburn had been one of the Whiz Kids. Whenever Roberts pitched that spring, Ashburn would arrange a telephone hookup with the ballpark and keep us listeners apprised of how his old buddy was doing. "After five innings in Lancaster," Ashburn would say, "Robin Roberts has given up two runs and three hits, and Reading leads the ballgame, 4-2."

I saw Roberts one more time. Reading was in the old Eastern League and so was York, where my mother grew up, and where her mother still lived. The York White Roses. Their big rival was Lancaster, the Red Roses. My grandmother's house was a couple of miles from the ballpark, which was an old-fashioned, run-of-the-mill country ballpark at the edge of town — cement grandstands in the open air, spindly light towers, outfield fences plastered with local advertising. Pesky remembers it. He managed Lancaster for a couple of seasons, and he remembers coming over by bus, the hilly farm country and the mile-wide Susquehanna River. I waited till Reading played in York, and went to visit grandmother.

We went to the ballgame, she and I, on a Saturday afternoon drenched in the daffodil light of May. You could smell the black earth of that rich farmland, turned inside-out for spring. The day was cool, just right. My grandmother and I arrived a few minutes before game time and sat behind the visitors' dugout. Robin Roberts wasn't pitching that day, but I was determined to see him, one way or another. I'd ridden a train and then a bus, and I was going to see the man. So, before the game started I took a deep breath and worked my way down to the dugout. A fat usher was relaxing by the barrier. I asked him if Robin Roberts was in the dugout.

"Maybe," the usher said.

"Would you please tell him I'm here?"

"Tell him who is here?"

I gave my name.

"Go sit down," the usher said, "I'll tell him."

I noticed, coming back up, that I was being stared at. There were a lot of kids. Kids with their ball gloves. I sat down beside my grandmother. She looked at me, smiling in a querying way she had. She remained tall all her life and sat up very straight. A grandmother who took all her grandchildren to Europe and who liked baseball.

"Well?" she said.

"I don't know," I said. For one thing, my last name would mean nothing to Roberts. And I didn't trust that usher.

The York White Roses broke onto the field to a festive cheer from the small, minor-league crowd. Reading's leadoff hitter strutted to the plate. There was, I remember, a lot of swagger on those double-A teams. The ballplayers must have all figured they were headed for the big leagues in a couple of years; they were just kids and full of themselves. The game began, and my heart sank lower and lower. The usher lolled against the dugout and wouldn't look at me.

The half inning ended. The Reading guys spilled up out of the dugout, and then a head and shoulders appeared above the dugout roof: Robin Roberts, squinting up to see who, exactly, had sent the message. I shot to my feet. This was a small grandstand, no higher than bleachers overlooking the football field of some rustic high school. Roberts didn't have any trouble spotting me. He didn't look at all surprised, just beckoned me with a toss of his head.

He met me at the barrier. We shook hands.

"You didn't come all this way to see a minor-league ballgame, did you?" he said.

"My grandmother lives here," I said. "I'm visiting her."

"Ah," he said, as if relieved.

His gaze was straying past me, to the crowd in the sunshine. He looked anxious, looked almost afraid of what he might see up there. He wore a regular Phillies road uniform. I suppose the club couldn't afford its own uniforms, or at least preferred to take leftovers from the parent big-league team.

"You're pitching well," I said.

"Oh," he said, in that wry, wistful way, "I'm gettin' a few of these boys out."

Boys. Yes. They were my age, and younger. And yet they had men's bodies, and an arrogant grace that was beyond me, unimaginable. They were a little more than boys to me, and I didn't understand, then, Robin's discomfort, a nervousness that had worked its way into his easygoing face.

He was uncomfortable standing there talking to me; I didn't know why, exactly. I was sure it was only a matter of time before he'd be pitching for the Phillies.

"Curt had a nice game the other day," I said. Simmons had beaten Pittsburgh. They'd scored five runs off him, but he'd stayed in there and gotten the win.

Robin said, "Curt did?"

"He beat the Pirates," I said.

"Oh, yeah."

Play was resuming. Robin glanced over his shoulder toward the plate. Apparently they would play ball with him standing here. This was double A, and he was Robin Roberts. But I knew he wanted to sit down. He wanted to vanish; I sensed that much.

"Listen," I said, "maybe I could see you when you come to Pawtucket this summer. I don't live far from there."

Pawtucket then was in the Eastern League. It's all been changed. The old Eastern League is gone.

"All right," he said, without enthusiasm.

"Unless you're up with the Phillies," I said.

"You could write to me," he said. "Care of the ballclub."

I said I would. I wished him luck.

"Thanks," he said.

It hit me finally that he looked tired. Not old, just tired. We shook hands.

"Good luck," I said again.

"Thanks for comin' by," he said.

I turned, climbed the cement steps. People stared. Kids. One kid at the end of a row asked me, "Are you a ballplayer?"

"No," I said, "I'm a friend of Robin Roberts."

I did write to him after I got home for the summer. It must have been mid-June. I didn't get an answer for a long time, till I began to think he'd had enough of me. I supposed he had better things to do in Pawtucket than have dinner with me. But in July, I heard from him. I have the letter, of course. It is written in ballpoint on stationary with his name, Robin E. Roberts, printed at the top, and a leafy-sounding address in Meadowbrook, Pennsylvania. Time has rubbed smoky brownish smudges into the paper. The ballpoint ink has bled to a lead-gray. *"Dear John,"* he writes,

> *Thank you for taking the time to write. I don't believe I'll be in Pawtucket for quite a while.*
>
> *Good luck to you. Hope you are a very successful writer. I'm in fine health and so is my family.*
>
> *Ballplayers are just people. We play a boy's game all our lives. I'm finding it extremely difficult to separate myself from this boy's game. It's been good to me.*
>
> *Good luck, Robin.*

1988

ε♣

Footnote:
From Voices from Cooperstown by Anthony J. Connor

ROBIN ROBERTS

I have four sons, and when my wife asked me about Little League, I told her, "No way in the world." And most professional athletes feel that way about kids under fourteen. If you try to make it serious before they're physically able to handle what they're doing, you run into all sorts of problems.

Generally in the Little League you're up against a good pitcher who throws like hell. What does the coach say? Get a walk. Isn't that beautiful way to learn to hit? For four years you stand up there looking for a walk.

Baseball at that age should be a softball thrown overhand where a boy can hit fifteen times a game, with no walks and strikeouts. They should be running and sliding into bases. The score should be 42-38.

I certainly would never let my boys enter a league where they'd be throwing curves at eight- or nine-year-olds. And I wouldn't want them all steamed up, heading for a pennant playoff at eleven, or a World Series at twelve. My father encouraged me to take it easy, and at eighteen I had an arm prepared for the strain of real pitching.

1982

Leigh Montville

🙢

From Citizen Ryan

The last forty-five minutes of Texas twilight have arrived. The day has been gray anyway, cool, and now the colors begin to fade even further as the unseen sun dips toward the trees at the edge of the pasture. The birds know that night is coming. Hear them squawk? The horses have to be fed. They stand in a group, five of them, behind a brown three-board fence. Waiting. A car passes on the road in the distance. Another. Men coming home from work. Women bringing their children from late practices and meetings at the high school.

"Curveball," Nolan Ryan says.

He stands in the middle of the pasture. This is farmland. The horses have galloped across it and tractors and trucks have been driven across it, and the grass is all knobby and clumpy, certainly unmowed, and yet...He is at the base of a little grass-covered mound. Mound? His neighbor Harry Spilman, chewing a touch of tobacco, is crouched behind a patch of white that shows through the grass. A patch of white?

Nolan tucks his left leg into his chest and accelerates off his right leg and throws the baseball. Harry does not have to move his mitt.

"Good one," Harry says.

There is a rusted chain-link fence, twelve feet high, a few feet behind Harry. Fence? There is the twelve-foot-high fence and the patch of white in front of Harry and the mound in back of Nolan and ... yes, sure. The mind and the eye simultaneously bring out the recessed image of a diamond, as if they were solving a puzzle in the Sunday comics. "I built it for my son when he was in Little League," Nolan says. "Little Leaguers never have a place to practice. I built it and they used it for a couple of years. Then I let it all go back. Watch where you walk." He fingers the baseball in his hand.

"Straight," he says.

Nolan's three dogs are fanned out in what could be loosely called an outfield alignment. That is Buster in left and Suzy in center and fat old Bea in right. The fourth dog, tied in the back of the pickup in the driveway, the dog that is barking, is Harry's dog Sarge. Sarge simply can't control himself. Let him loose and he becomes too excited. He chases the ball wherever it goes. He tries to grab it straight out of Nolan's or Harry's hand. Sarge has had a million second chances. Had one just today. Can't control himself. Back in the truck.

"There was something on that pitch," Harry says a second after the ball arrives. "It was traveling."

The first time Nolan was in this field, let's see, he was with the Girl Scouts. Camping with the Girl Scouts. His mother, Martha, was a troop leader, and she wasn't going to let her youngest child, seven years old, stay home while she was taking those girls for a night of outdoor adventure at Mr. Evans' ranch. This was back in 1954, when the bayou over there wasn't straight, before the widening was done and the lake was formed at the other end and the tract development came. Let's see. There were more trees then. The road out there wasn't even a road. There was another road. Yes. Another road. Smaller. A back road. A further-back road.

"Change-up," Nolan says.

He is still here. How many years later? The land now is his, acquired thirteen years ago in a straight trade, a new house that Nolan owned for Mr. Evans' old house and the land. This is a Tuesday, late in February. The game of pitch and catch has been taking place almost every night for a month. Same time. Same place. Training camp is eight days away, and the fastballs are becoming faster and the curveballs are becoming curvier. A stranger, out on the road, might look and squint and see only a couple of middle-aged guys in the middle of nowhere trying to find a few Absorbine, Jr. memories, but there really aren't many strangers out there on the road. These are familiar people. A horn honks. Another. There's old Nolan, tossing with Harry. Getting ready.

"Looked good," Harry says.

"I don't know," Nolan says. "That one might have got hit."

The shades of gray darken, and Nolan is working just a little harder tonight. He has to miss the workout tomorrow. Has to go to the White House. To see the President. Up there in Washington. He will be back in Alvin, Texas, back here, Thursday.

"I don't know how he does it," says Kim Spilman, Nolan's secretary and Harry's wife. "The letters, the invitations, the demands. The businesses. There always is someone who wants him to be a grand marshal in a parade, to talk at Career Day. Something. The White House. How do you stay normal with all of these people pulling at you all of the time? And yet he does it. God, he does. He's everything a person would want to be. He talks with my kids and he's just so nice. They'll ask me, 'Is he supposed to be famous or some-thing?' That's just how he is."

The White House is the latest thing. The White House. The war in the Persian Gulf is at its hottest stretch. The coalition airplanes are pounding Baghdad with their bombs. The ground war will start in four more days. The White House is on television seventeen times every day. The President is seen going from meeting to press conference to late night strategy session. In the midst of all this, the Queen and Prince Consort of Denmark are invited for dinner. Nolan and his wife, Ruth, also are invited for dinner. They are also invited to stay overnight. At the White House.

When will it all stop?

The drumbeat of celebrity always has been in the back-ground — good pitcher, fastest fastball going, All-Star — but in the past two years, since Nolan went to the Texas Rang-ers, it has become louder and louder. The 5,000th strikeout was a jump in 1989. A record. The sixth no-hitter, spun in Oakland in June of last year against the then-world-cham-pion Athletics, was another jump. Another record. The 300th win, in July, was a capper. How noisy can noisy be for an essentially quiet person practicing a physical craft? The line has shot off the graph paper. The White House.

"Nolan was here when the call came," Kim says in the office Nolan has rented in the Merchants Bank in Alvin to handle the increased demands on his life. "It's funny how that works. As soon as he gets here, the phone starts ring-ing of the hook. It's like people have antennae or something to tell them he's here. I took the call, and the message was something like, 'Please stay on the line for the President of the United States.' I was so excited I ran into the bank to tell everyone that Nolan was being invited to the White House."

There is the crazy thought that maybe George Bush is going to call this forty-four-year-old man into the Oval Office and ask him to take a quick trip to the Middle East. Let Saddam Hussein find an emissary to send from Iraq, a solid citizen, someone who represents all the best qualities of Iraqi culture. Let him talk to Nolan, the American representative, to straighten out all of this feuding and fighting. There is the crazy thought that this would not be so crazy. Who would be better?

"I don't know how it is in the rest of the country," Jim Stinson, Nolan's longtime friend and business partner, says, "but in Texas he is bigger than John Wayne right now. And you will wear out a truck finding someone who's nicer than Nolan Ryan."

John Wayne?

"I talk with ad agencies about him," Matt Merola, Nolan's longtime agent from New York, says. "They will say, 'Well, can he talk?' I will tell them if they're looking for Sir Laurence Olivier, they'd better go to Central Casting. But if they're looking for someone who is honest, who is sincere, who can talk about things in his way — Jimmy Stewart. If they are looking for Jimmy Stewart, they want Nolan. He is someone who is really real."

Jimmy Stewart?

In the tie-a-yellow-ribbon Americanism of the nineties, Nolan somehow has become the perfect oak tree. The fact that he still can compete with the young and wild-eyed millionaires of his game and still can make them look silly is only the beginning. He is Citizen Ryan, a total package. Tired of the fatheads who spend their first paychecks on sports cars that run on airplane fuel? Seen too much of the substance abusers and late night carousers and the uncoachable prima donnas? Here is a family man. Here is a businessman. Here is a cowboy. Here is Nolan Ryan, cut from a good bolt of denim cloth and served with a glass of milk and no apologies.

"Do you know what he has?" says Terry Koch-Bostic of the Slater-Hanft-Martin advertising agency in New York, which signed Ryan as the spokesman for Bic razors in 1990, "He was the real stuff of real heroes, the kind of heroes that maybe we've been missing for the last three decades. That's the kind of guy he is. When we were making our deal, his first consideration was his family. He said that money was not important, that he couldn't be traveling around in the off-season. He wanted to be home. I told that to Mr. [Bruno] Bich and he said, 'Well, yes, that's exactly the kind of guy we want. A person whose family comes first. Absolutely.'"

ॐ

After twenty-three years, the man still is married to his high school sweetheart, and Ruth remembers when a big date simply was watching him take target practice with his .22 pistol. They still live in the same town and their kids attend the same schools they attended. A big night still is a trip to Baskin-Robbins for ice cream. A big Saturday night still is dancing the two-step with friends at Eddie's Country Ballroom. Pretty good two-step, too.

A workday is a workday. Vacations still are mostly for other people, although there were three days at the end of last year in Las Vegas for the National Finals Rodeo. There is no real "off" in the off-season. Nolan is a rancher. Nolan owns three ranches. The biggest, China Grove, in Rosharon, near Alvin, has 550 mama cows and 33 bulls and as many as 1,100 head, total, at the end of calving season, which is just about now. Relaxation is riding a horse and penning the calves and doing a cattle rancher's hard work.

"He's a hands-on owner, for sure," Larry McKim, the ranch manager, says. "When he comes here, he gets right into it. He helps us castrate the steers, dehorn 'em, every-thing. Nothing fazes him. I'll see him reach into the chute with that million-dollar right arm and I'll say to myself, 'Are you sure you want to do that?' But he'll never buckle. He'll go right in there."

"Nolan is as good a cattleman as there is in the state of Texas," Stinson, a partner in China Grove, says. "He's stride for stride with all of 'em. If he'd never picked up a baseball, he'd still be a great success as a cattleman. He's been doing it all his life. I remember his mother telling me once how he saved up enough money when he was a kid to buy four calves. He lived in town, so he had to raise 'em in the garage. Fed 'em all from a baby bottle."

The banking business is another long-term affair. Nolan made news last year when he purchased the Danbury State Bank, about ten miles from Alvin, but he had been on the board of directors of an Alvin bank for ten years. Again, he was not just a name on the letterhead. He worked. He sat in on loan meetings. He formulated bank policy. He preached moderation. He still is one of those guys who travel the extra mile for gas at $1.06 per gallon if the local station is charging $1.10. The word is frugal. He did not rush into a deal that translated into "dumb baseball player buys failing bank." He waited and learned, and moved at the proper time.

"I'd use another word for him, 'tight,'" Sonny Corley, president of the Danbury bank, says. "But that's all right, because I'm tight, too. I think he got a great deal here, because under the bank's charter he can expand anywhere in the state of Texas. Nolan knows what he's doing. He's been in the banking business for a while, and he has a great ability to look at a situation and analyze it. He has what I'd call country smarts. Nolan has great country smarts."

His final off-season occupation is being Nolan Ryan. This has become the most demanding job of them all. Until the past two years, his endorsements mostly were local and regional — Whataburger and Bizmart office supplies — but now he shaves for Bic and takes Advil for headaches and wears Wrangler jeans over his Justin boots when he goes out for a western-wear night. He could sign baseballs forever for charity, especially across the "sweet spot" in the front of the ball, which immediately increases its value. He does not do the autograph shows, signing for money. He does not do speeches for money, but he does talk for certain charities he considers important. The requests are so numerous now that mail arrives at his office in tubs from the Alvin post office. He and Ruth used to handle the mail at home. The tubs began to take control. He has added the office and secretary in the past two years.

"Can you imagine that they did all this at home?" Kim says as Ruth arrives at the office with another tub. "The letters he gets. The requests — he could speak every night of the year if he wanted. Somewhere."

His strength is that he does not go somewhere every night. He usually goes home. The increase in Nolan's celebrity has come at a good time, because his oldest son, Reid, nineteen, is a freshman at the University of Texas in Austin, and his other children, Reese, fifteen, and Wendy, fourteen, are in high school, and his days are free. But he wants to be home for dinner. That is his base. He creates his own orbit around the base, and the orbit rarely leaves Texas in the off-season. He will travel to Arlington Stadium for a day, knock off a series of commitments there and come home. He will go to Abilene or Austin and come home. He works and then he comes home.

"He's just such an unassuming, fine guy," Stinson says. "I called him the day after he pitched the no-hitter last year. We talked for half an hour. He never mentioned the no-hitter. Finally, I had to mention it. He said, 'Yeah, I had it going pretty good.' That's it."

"We had to follow him around a bit during the season to complete the [Bic] commercial," Koch-Bostic at the ad agency says. "We finally did it in Los Angeles. He was coming off the disabled list with a bad back. I was thinking about his bad back. The next game, his second start, he's in Oakland, throwing the no-hitter. Reese is rubbing his back in the Ranger dugout between innings."

"The thing I like about him is not so much what he does but the way he does it," McKim says at the ranch. "The only thing fast about him is his fastball. He's so calm, so good-natured, so easy. He's the best rancher I've ever worked for. The other ones were pretty hyper, pretty nervous, always concerned with money. Nolan, he's a people person, not a money person."

The money matters, but it doesn't matter that much. Merola, the agent, tells clients they can have "the sizzle or the steak." Nolan is the steak, and steak is popular. He was asked to run for Texas agriculture commissioner last year, thought about it because he was opposed to what he considered the incumbent's anticattleman policies, but finally decided he didn't have the time. The candidate he endorsed, Rick Perry, beat the incumbent, Jim Hightower, in a surprise. The Texas Senate just passed a bill to have a stretch of Highway 288 near Alvin renamed the Nolan Ryan Expressway. There are plans in Alvin to build a Nolan Ryan Museum. Every day there seem to be offers from somewhere to do something involving Nolan. Every day Nolan gives them a look.

He takes his time. Always.

"The big thing with Nolan is that he's hard to pin down," Kim says. "He doesn't like to schedule things in advance because he never knows what's going to come up. Especially with the kids. If Reese or Wendy has a game or something, he'd like to go. If you do pin him down, though, he'll be where he's supposed to be. You can count on it."

The invitation to the White House was typical. Kim came back into the office, still excited at the news. Nolan said he couldn't go. He had looked at his schedule and found he had promised to speak to a cattlemen's civic group in Cotulla to raise scholarships. That was that. Kim told him he was crazy. He said he had turned down trips to the White House in the past. There always seemed to be something.

"Look," Kim said, "if you called the people in Cotulla and said you were invited to the White House, I'm sure they'd understand. They could just schedule you for another night."

"You do it," Nolan said.

The people in Cotulla understood. Duty called for Citizen Ryan. John Wayne, maybe Jimmy Stewart, had to be at the White House. He would appear in Cotulla the next week if he wasn't in the Middle East.

Nolan and Harry talk while they throw the ball back and forth in the pasture. Harry is not exactly the average next-door recruit, some accountant who bought himself a baseball glove just to help the famous pitcher get ready. Not at all. Harry played too, twelve years of scuffling on the fringes of four different teams in the major leagues and six in the minors. He is thirty-seven years old now, and he retired with bad knees at the end of the last season, which he spent with the Houston Astros' Triple A team in Tucson. He will be working this year as roving hitting coach in the Cleveland Indians' minor-league system.

"So Roger Clemens is getting five million dollars," Nolan says, shaking his head. "If Roger's worth five million, what's Wade Boggs going to be worth?"

Straight fastball.

Splat!

"What about Jim Deshaies?" Harry says. "He's making two million — something. He won seven games last year. Seven games and he's making two million. Isn't that something?"

Curveball.

Splat!

"I know one thing," Nolan says. "I'd like to be about twenty-five years old now and have about five thousand innings ahead of me."

Change-up.

Perfect.

Harry remembers the first time he saw Nolan pitch, in 1980. Harry was playing with the Cincinnati Reds, and Nolan, after eight years with the California Angels, had just arrived back in the National League with the Astros. It was an occasion, seeing the great fireballer for the first time. Harry had a great seat on the bench. He really wanted to see the first confrontation between Nolan and Johnny Bench. Everyone did. Bench dug in at the plate. Nolan stared from the mound. All the players moved to the far edges of their seats. Nolan threw a slow, lazy curveball that bounced about a foot and a half in front of the plate. Bench swung so hard that the temperature must have dropped 5 degrees in the ballpark. A curveball! Beautiful.

Harry soon moved along to the Astros himself, and that was where he became friends with Nolan. Harry is from Dawson, Georgia, so he is another small-town southern guy who talks with the accent. He has the same likes and values as Nolan. He likes to hunt. He likes to fish. He likes horses and riding and, of course, talking baseball. When it came time to decide where he would live in the off-season and the rest of his life, Harry picked Alvin, even though he had moved to the San Francisco Giants. Nolan worked out a deal for the land and house next door. What could be better? In the other years, when they were both playing, Nolan would throw batting practice to Harry down at the high school. Batting practice from Nolan Ryan. What could be better? Kim works for Nolan. Harry works with Nolan. Harry is one of the ten current or former teammates who have named a son after Nolan. Everybody is friends.

In the big leagues, Harry faced Nolan twice. The first time, Harry hit a homer, a grand feat considering Harry had only eighteen homers lifetime. The second time, Nolan struck out Harry on a high, 3-2 fastball. Then, again, there is an argument about this.

"When Nolan got his five thousandth strikeout, *USA Today* ran a list of all the guys he'd struck out in his career," Harry says. "I looked for my name. I wasn't there, I say it never happened. Nolan even checked with the Rangers public relations department. They said there must have been a mistake, because I pinch-hit. I say it never happened."

"It happened," Nolan says.

"Not if my name isn't on the list," Harry says. (It is now. The 1991 Rangers media guide lists Harry as one of Nolan's victims.)

Curveball.

Splat!

The workout began in the driveway. Nolan stretched and then started throwing a football with Harry, long and straight spirals. This is part of the conditioning process encouraged by Rangers pitching coach Tom House. Nolan had told House two years ago, his first day as a Ranger, that he hoped House wouldn't be upset if he didn't throw the football with everyone else. House said a sure-bet Hall of Famer could do what he wanted. One week passed and then two weeks and then Nolan suddenly was throwing the football. He did what he does with everything. He studied the concept. He decided for himself. He threw the football. No big deal. He liked the mechanics. He liked the way the motion loosened his arm and shoulder. Logic. He threw the football.

"We're finding it's harder than it looks," Nolan says.

"Maybe we remember ourselves being better than we were," Harry says. "I thought I could throw that thing in high school."

Nolan played two years of football in junior high and one year in high school. He was an end. His biggest memory is of an eighth-grade scrimmage down at Danbury, where he owns the bank. The farm boys at Danbury were so poor they didn't even have shoes. Didn't have shoes! The Danbury coach said it wouldn't be fair if his team didn't have shoes and the other team did, so the Alvin coach had his players take off their shoes. No matter. Who couldn't beat a team that was so poor the players didn't have shoes? Danbury killed Alvin, 42-0. Nolan quit football after the next year. Stinson begged Nolan to stay because he thought Nolan would help the team. Help the team? Stinson says now that "Jim Thorpe couldn't have helped that team." Stinson and Nolan laugh about that.

"I liked basketball," Nolan says. "I could play a little. I could dunk."

After throwing the football, Nolan and Harry threw a baseball in the driveway for a while. Easy tosses. After that, Nolan put on his blue Rangers cleats to throw out in the pasture. Hard tosses. The workout began a little before five o'clock, and now the time is a little after six. The light is almost gone. The dogs have lost interest, running into the woods in what would be dead center field. Nolan says, "They're probably looking for yesterday's game ball." A pitcher's grim joke. Think about it. Nolan says this is the kind of light he wouldn't mind having for all baseball games all of the time. Think about it. He asks Harry if there is enough light for one more pitch. Harry says that there is.

"Straight," Nolan says.

Splat!

"The funniest thing, to me, is when we drive by the Bizmart billboard," Ruth Ryan says. "There's one on the Gulf Freeway and there's one on the freeway in Austin and one in Arlington. They're huge. You look up and there's Nolan. Thirty feet high. I look up, every time, and I say, 'This isn't real.' The kids always start to make fun of him."

There wasn't any grand plan for him to play this long. There wasn't any grand plan for him to become this famous. There wasn't even any grand plan for him to lead a life that would be held up as model for family men everywhere. Everything sort of evolved. Happened. Nolan figured he would pitch for four years or five and then his arm would go dead and he would come home and maybe begin school and become a veterinarian. Or maybe not. Ruth remembers wondering fifteen years ago, when he was with the Angels and was having arm surgery, if he ever would throw a baseball again.

One pitch somehow was followed by another pitch and then another. One family crisis led to the next crisis. There was a balancing act that somehow led across a high wire to here. Twenty-six years of professional baseball. Twenty-six years of living. Twenty-six years?

"I was watching a television show the other night," Nolan says. "Carol Burnett was hosting a special about *The Ed Sullivan Show*. I remembered I was on *The Ed Sullivan Show*. With the Mets, when we won it in 1969. We all came on together and sang some song."

He has survived, he figures, on a combination of luck and work and those country smarts. He studied what he did, studied from the beginning. He remembers the first time he ever sat in a big-league clubhouse, just a kid, up for a moment in 1966. The Mets were still an expansion team, filled with older rejects from established teams. He remembers the old-timers just coasting, taking the paycheck, gliding out the door as effortlessly as possible. He remembers thinking to himself that he would never do that. He never has.

"I figured things out for myself," he says. "I always wanted to keep in shape, especially after I turned thirty. I always had my workouts. I started lifting weights in 1972. Nobody was doing that back then. They told you not to lift weights. I thought it would help me. The older I got, the more I worked out…to the point now that I work out more than anyone on our team. I have to do it. To compete with kids who are half your age, you have to do a whole lot more than they do."

He stuck with three pitches. Fastball. Curve. Change. The fastball began to slow about ten years ago, but not enough to make hitters comfortable. The curve improved. The change-up improved a lot. He stayed away from the slider, a pitch he always has thought is a killer of arms. In California, Angel coach Marv Grissom tried to get him to throw the slider. Nolan nodded, said he would try it out. He never really tried. Never wanted to take that chance.

The Rangers' pitching coach, House, is sort of a New Age baseball experimentalist. He uses computers, tests pitching theories. He finds again and again that Nolan figured out this business in his head before the computers did. Nolan, for instance, will mention that he thinks if his back is loose and his left leg is extended just a little higher, his fastball will be better. House will test the proposition on the computer. Whir and hum. Nolan is right again.

"I sometimes think he's the only one who understands me," House says. "He's my translator. He takes what I'm saying in scientific language and puts it into English for the rest of the guys. He'll say, 'This is what he's saying...' Everyone else will start nodding his head."

The idea of staying in Alvin never really came to debate. Why not stay? Isn't this where everyone we know always has lived? The idea of staying married never came to debate. Why not? Isn't that what you're supposed to do? The idea of raising a family was ingrained. Wasn't that what our parents did? Raise families? One year had led into another. Last year, Nolan and Ruth went to the twenty-fifth reunion of the Alvin High class of 1965. Everyone hung out at Dairyland on Friday night, the way they had in school. There was a dance at the country club on Saturday night, a picnic on Sunday.

"He is the one who has kept everything together," Ruth says. "Him. It would be so easy for him to go off, to just say, 'You take care of the kids while I go do this business.' He never says that. He always tries to make us a part of everything. He is going to Abilene on business this weekend. He could just go. He doesn't want that. He wants us with him."

"I think you learn so much more from your parents than you ever thought possible," Nolan says. "It just comes through. I find it comes through again and again."

The lessons of long ago do not leave. How can he go to the gym early every morning of the year, to the free weights and torture machines inside a little room he built off his barn? How can he fight through the everyday soreness, refuse to stay in bed just once? How can he be strong when his body wants to turn soft? How can he do all that work in the morning and then be throwing at night? He remembers delivering newspapers with his father as a boy. His father had two jobs. Nolan would have to get up at one o'clock in the morning, roll the papers for an hour, then deliver them around the back roads of Alvin, fifty-five miles of traveling until four. Then he would go back to bed for a few more hours of sleep before school. Every day.

"You had the feeling that people were counting on you," he says. "If you didn't get up, they weren't going to get their papers. You just did it. You had a sense of responsibility. I guess I never lost it. There are a lot of mornings where I'd just like to keep my dead butt in bed. I just get up."

He says he is so old that he remembers when baseball wasn't the fast road to wealth that it has become. He says he made $7,000 in his first major-league season. When the Mets won the World Series in 1969, his share of the winnings tripled his basic salary. He bought his first house. For ten years, playing baseball was an economic struggle. He remembers installing air conditioners in the off-season. Pumping gas. There weren't always ranches and banks and endorsements.

"I talk about some of this stuff sometimes and kids in the clubhouse look at me as if I'm sort of a codger," he says. "And I guess I am. I look at these kids on our team — we have a young team — and I'm the same age as most of their fathers. I'm like one of the coaches. That's how old I am. The one thing, I think, that age has given me is a sense of history. I see a lot of the young guys and the money they make, and they don't know what went into getting that money. That sort of bothers me. It makes you think about a lot of things we just take for granted."

He remembers a time when there was no television in his house, when he would stand in the dark of Dezo Drive and look through neighbors' windows at this miraculous invention. He remembers his grandmother had outdoor plumbing. Man walking on the moon? He remembers long before that. A bus was taking him to play some game in eighth grade in Houston. The coach pointed out the window and said that a thing called NASA was going to be built in a vacant field they were passing. Cows were in the middle of the field. NASA.

"You think sometimes about all the stuff that has happened," he says. "I was reading somewhere the other day that the Rural Electrification Act is fifty years old. Fifty years ago, people were just getting electricity. Thirty years after that, man was walking on the moon."

He says he has no goals for how long he will pitch. The last few years have been a wonderful bonus. He will pitch this year and see what happens. His wife has a hunch that this will be his last year, but it is only a hunch. His friends think he will pitch as long as he is healthy and successful. House thinks, crazy as it sounds, that Nolan is pitching as well now as he ever did. House thinks Nolan will pitch as long as Nolan wants to pitch, as long as he wants to make the physical sacrifices to fight the aging process.

After that, politics is always a possibility, but Nolan says he will not go looking in that direction. He simply will listen if someone talks. The ranching business always has been interesting. The banking business is turning out to be very interesting. He has plans for expansion. The Danbury bank has grown in less than a year from a $9 million bank to a $13 million bank. Maybe he'll do something in baseball. The baseball business certainly has been interesting.

"I remember going to Houston to watch the old .45s play at Colt Stadium," Nolan says. "I went with my dad, I guess. I remember saying, 'How about this? These guys get paid to play baseball.' I said, 'Look at this guy over here, he doesn't even get to play in the game and he still gets paid.' Then, that's what I did. Played baseball for money. It's funny. I go to the career days at high schools and I tell kids that playing baseball isn't a career. It really isn't. How many players ever make the major leagues, and how long do they stay if they make it? I think the average is something like five years. I tell kids they should plan to do something else, really, with their lives...and yet, here I am. I've been in it this long, and the last two years, I have to say, have been the highlight."

"His age has brought him all this attention," Ruth says, "and I really think he has earned it. I think people looked past him for a long time. I remember being really aggravated back in 1973 when he didn't win the Cy Young Award and I really thought he deserved it. I remember hearing some mean things that people would say. About him being just a .500 pitcher. He would always say that everyone is entitled to an opinion. I would get mad. So now I get a lot of satisfaction from the accolades he's getting. He deserves them all."

Harry and Nolan walk out of the pasture carrying their gloves. Harry unties Sarge at last from the back of the pickup, and Sarge barks and runs around like the strange dog he is. Reese, who is in the ninth grade, is home from a baseball scrimmage. He drove the old farm-only truck to the lake and back to check his six trout lines. They were empty. Crabs had eaten the bait. He is talking, talking, a teenager in a rush. That is Reese. He picks up the football and starts throwing it with Harry.

"I'd be a great quarterback," Reese says. "I was the quarterback in seventh grade. You should have seen me. I was awesome. Just awesome. You should have seen me last year, eighth grade, when I was a Tower of Power free safety. Awesome."

"How'd practice go today?" Nolan asks.

"I got hit in the shin."

"You got hit in the chin?"

"The shin. It hurt."

"Did you pitch any?"

"Yes, sir. I pitched to five batters. One kid...I threw the ball behind him."

"Uh-huh," Harry says. "Like father, like son."

In the house, Ruth can be seen through the lighted kitchen window, moving around the cabinets. She went through the day in a buzz, picking up the tickets to Washington, packing the bags for the White House. She bought a new pleated shirt for Nolan to wear with his tuxedo because the old one looked a little too shabby for dinner with the Queen and Prince of Denmark, not to mention President Bush. She picked up her new dress, a long gown bought in Houston, from her mother's house. Her mother had sewn the hem.

Nolan still has to feed the horses and Harry will help him, but there is a moment here, a pause. It is the pause at the end of the normal working day. It is the pause at the end of a workout, the job done, the sweat still fresh. It is the reward. Night is here, and there is a fine sense of fulfillment. This is life. This is breathing. This is it. Friends and family and dogs and home and land. Dinner soon to arrive.

Nolan leans on the fender of his wife's car, resting. He is wearing a cap from a feed company, a dark blue windbreaker and a pair of blue gym-instructor sweatpants. He could be anybody. Just a middle-aged, middle-of-the-road anybody. He looks across his pasture with its subliminal baseball field, and someone points out the similarity of the scene to ones in the baseball movie *Field of Dreams*. See the woods? Isn't that where Shoeless Joe Jackson should emerge, ready to play baseball with the other immortals? What was the line?

If you build it, he will come.

"I built it," Nolan says. "He never came. Maybe I should have put in lights."

Tomorrow, the White House.

1991

Tom Verducci

ℯ❧

From Once in a Lifetime

The best right-handed pitcher born in the past 100 years walks among us today. His career is a masterpiece, available for all to see every fifth day or so as he works atop the pitching mounds of National League ballparks. The rest of us, should we recognize our good fortune, could be eyewitnesses to genius. Did you see van Gogh paint? No, you could respond, but I saw Greg Maddux pitch.

Or maybe you haven't noticed, which is precisely the way Gregory Alan Maddux of the Atlanta Braves would prefer it. He is as consistent as a metronome and, to the casual eye, about as exciting. Despite his unprepossessing frame, he has won three consecutive National League Cy Young Awards and is a virtual lock to win his fourth, with a 12-1 record and a league-leading 1.74 ERA at week's end. Yet Maddux still doesn't have a single major endorsement deal. He is the wallflower who begged out of starting last month's All-Star Game, thus allowing baseball's 1995 media sensation, Hideo Nomo, to start in his place. Maddux's claim that he had a slight leg injury smelled fishier than yesterday's sushi, but it allowed him to stay comfortably in the shadows, away from the national spotlight.

"A hitter will get, say, 600 at bats over a year," Maddux says. "He may see me only six or seven times out of those 600. I'm not going to do anything or say anything that makes him remember me."

"It's amazing," says fellow Brave hurler John Smoltz, "that in this day and age he's kept such a low profile after all he's done. He doesn't want you to figure him out. If you don't know where he's coming from, he's got you."

What sets Maddux apart is an analytical, Pentium-quick mind that constantly processes information no one else sees. At home in Las Vegas he is a formidable poker player, detecting when an opponent has a good hand by the way he strokes his chin or suddenly stops fiddling with his chips. Maddux uses a numerical system in his head that tells him when to stand and when to hit at the blackjack table. But he is even better at analyzing hitters — so good that four times this year, while seated next to Smoltz in the dugout, he has warned, "This guy's going to hit a foul ball in here." Three of those times a foul came screeching into the dugout.

If his radar is that sensitive while kicking back in the dugout, imagine the clues he uncovers while bearing down on the mound. Says teammate Tom Glavine, the last National Leaguer to win the Cy Young Award before Maddux made it his personal property, "I think he's got a gift. He's able to notice things in the course of a game that no one else can — the way a hitter may open up a little, move up in the box an inch, change his stance. I've tried to be aware of that stuff. I really have. But I'm so focused on what *I'm* trying to do. I don't know how he does it."

This seeming omniscience is complemented by Maddux's mastery of the subtle side of pitching: the movement and location of his pitches. That's how he can dominate without a signature pitch, without anything close to the menace of Bob Gibson's fastball or the treachery of Sandy Koufax's curve. "The more you know about baseball, the more you appreciate Greg Maddux," says Jim Guadagno, who compiles the Braves' statistical data bases. "He gets away with stuff nobody else does. You're always asking, 'How does he do it?' There is always this 10 percent that is the mystery of him. He likes that."

The mystery of Maddux. Maybe one percent of it gets peeled back with this fact he would rather you not know: Over the past four seasons Maddux has been the greatest right-handed pitcher since Walter Johnson, who was born in 1887 — so long ago that van Gogh, another chap whose prime passed without proper notice, was still alive.

No righthander has been this good for this long since the Dead Ball era ended in 1920, after which even Johnson, who had ERAs lower than 2.00 for 11 of his first 13 seasons, never again did better than 2.72. Since then, and assuming Maddux maintains something close to his current rate of efficiency for his last 10 or 11 starts of 1995, only two pitchers will have had four consecutive seasons with an ERA of 2.40 or better: Koufax (1963-66) and Maddux (1992-95). And Koufax had his run before the mound was lowered in 1969. What Maddux has done is put up Dead Ball numbers in a Rabbit Ball era.

You scoff. How could this guy who finished a game last month against the San Francisco Giants throwing 81-mph fastballs be better than Gibson, Bob Feller, Tom Seaver, Jim Palmer, or even Roger Clemens and Dwight Gooden? Because Maddux outshines them all when measured by the fairest means of comparing pitchers of different periods: individual ERA relative to league ERA. It sizes up a pitcher against his contemporaries, the pitchers who are facing the same hitters, over the same period of time.

For instance, Maddux's 1.56 ERA last season was more remarkable than Gibson's glitzier 1.12 mark of 1968. Why? Because Maddux did it when the National League ERA was 4.21, the fifth highest since earned run averages were first kept as an official stat in 1912. That means Maddux's ERA was only 37.1 percent of the league average. Gibson's extraordinary season occurred in 1968, when pitchers had such an easy time that the mound was lowered five inches the next year. The league ERA was 2.99, which puts Gibson's ERA percentage at 37.5.

Further, Maddux has put up four consecutive seasons in which his ERA was less than two thirds of his league's average: 62.3, 58.4, 37.1 and, at week's end, 41.9 percent. No right-hander since Johnson can match his four-year dominance.

"Koufax was the best pitcher I ever saw," says Dodger pitching coach Dave Wallace. "Maddux is right behind him with any of the other greats you want to name."

From 1963 to '66 the lefthanded Koufax put up the best four-year numbers of any pitcher in the past 75 years: 97-27 with a cumulative 1.86 ERA and four of his unmatched five straight ERA titles. He gave up fewer hits per nine innings than Maddux and had a better strikeouts-to-walks ratio. But measured at least one way, Maddux (gulp) compares favorably even with Koufax. His four-year ERA (2.02) is 51.1 percent of the league average over that time. Koufax's ERA was 53.1 percent of the league average. And Koufax worked in a better pitcher's park, Dodger Stadium, while Maddux has pitched all his home games in Chicago's Wrigley Field and Atlanta-Fulton County Stadium, two of the game's most notorious launching pads.

Maddux wins games, too. He is 68-28 over the past four years, a .708 winning percentage that exceeds the prime years of Feller, Gibson, Seaver, Palmer and Clemens. (Gooden, 73-26 beginning with 1984, had a four-year .737 mark.) He also rarely walks anyone (once every 10 1/3 innings this year); yields few home runs; and fields his position better than anyone else (a sixth Gold Glove is on its way). "Maddux is the best pitcher I ever saw," says Giants pitching coach Dick Pole, "because he does everything well. If you look up the word pitcher in a dictionary, his picture should be there."

❧

The best right-hander since Walter Johnson is eating a sandwich on the bed of his hotel room in Los Angeles and watching the Boston Red Sox play the Chicago White Sox on TV. An open suitcase is stuffed with more Nintendo games than clothes. With two days before his July 29 start in San Francisco, he has just returned from one of his frequent off-day workouts: 18 holes of golf. "I wouldn't consider myself a hard worker, but I'm not lazy," Maddux says. "I'm somewhere in the middle."

Rick Aguilera is pitching for Boston, and Maddux is calling pitches and location for him. Lance Johnson of the White Sox is late on a fastball, fouling it off to the left side.

"Aguilera knows by that swing that he can throw the fastball by him, so right here he's coming back with the splitter out of the strike zone," Maddux says. Aguilera throws the splitter but leaves it over the plate. Johnson slashes it for a single. "Right pitch," says Maddux, "he just made a mistake."

Though he has not seen the Giants since Opening Day, Maddux will not study videotapes of them. He doesn't bother watching tapes on the road. "Listen, it ain't nothin' like what people are saying and writing," he says of his reputation for meticulous study. "You want to know what my scouting report is?" He grabs a piece of paper off the nightstand. It is an alphabetized printout of career hits and at bats by Pittsburgh players against him. Maddux faced the Pirates in his previous start. He begins at the top of the list and from memory breaks down how he would pitch to each of their hitters.

"Look: Jay Bell, down and away; in to back him off. Jacob Brumfield: mix, will chase.... That's it. You can't go in with a script. You're always pitching off your last pitch. I don't think I understand hitting any better than I did four years ago. I'm just making better pitches at certain times."

It is getaway day. He closes the suitcase and wheels it out of the room toward the elevator. It tips over. He stands it up and pulls at it again. It falls again. He picks it up and resumes pulling. It falls. The suitcase is a scarred, mangled thing bearing a sticker of the Chicago Cubs, his former team. Isn't he due for a new bag? "No way," he says. "At the baggage carousel when everybody is looking for his Braves bag and they all look the same, they're going, 'Is that one mine? Is that mine?' Mine comes out, and I just walk over and pick it up." Classic Maddux. Always playing the percentages and always a step ahead of everybody else.

The previous day he did his only throwing off the mound between starts, removing his round-rimmed eyeglasses and handing them over to pitching coach Leo Mazzone before getting under way. (The other Brave starters throw twice between starts.) The session lasted only 10 minutes, going so well that Maddux giggled after one pitch.

Watch how most pitchers throw when they are working out between starts. They start from their full windup and often stay that way until a coach says, "OK, get some work in from the stretch." The first time Mazzone watched Maddux work out for the Braves, in 1993, he noticed that Maddux started from the stretch and threw most of his pitches that way. A little later Mazzone asked him, "Why do you do that?"

Replied Maddux, "The way I figure it, I'm going to have to make my best pitches out of the stretch."

"He has one of the brightest pitching minds I've ever been around," the pitching coach says, "including most coaches."

You would swear Maddux is a born pitcher until you hear him say, "When I was 15 years old I didn't think I was going to be a pitcher. I liked hitting." He was 16 when Rusty Medar, a volunteer coach in Las Vegas, watched the skinny kid throw straight over the top and told him, "You're probably never going to throw hard enough to overpower people." So the coach showed Maddux how to lower his arm and release the ball at what would be 10 o'clock on a clock face instead of 11 — and to switch from a four-seam fastball to a two-seamer. The ball immediately began to dance, usually down and away from a left-handed hitter. It is the same fastball he throws today. It is, he says, his best pitch, even if it only averages about 85 mph, 87 on a good day.

Maddux also throws a wonderfully disguised circle change-up, a cutter that bores in on the hands of lefthanded hitters, and two average breaking balls: a slider and curveball.

"I think he's gotten better even from when I faced him two years ago," says Braves catcher Charlie O'Brien, who batted against Maddux as a New York Met. "I've never seen so many guys leaving the plate saying. "Damn, how did he do that?'"

Maddux has also developed a bulletproof confidence in his pitches. "It keeps you from panicking," he says. He still vividly recalls the moment seven years ago when he realized he had to learn to trust his own abilities. He lost to St. Louis in the 11th inning when Luis Alicea hit one of his fastballs for a bad-hop, bases-loaded single. "I pitched 10 scoreless innings and lost because I was afraid to throw a change-up," he says.

"Now," says Pole, "if he gets a full count on you with the bases loaded, he'll throw a change-up. That s.o.b. doesn't even care about walking in the tying run."

When July 29 rolled around, Maddux beat the Giants 5-1 with a four-hitter. He threw a first-pitch strike to 24 of the 33 batters he faced and got 19 outs on ground balls and strikeouts. And yet because he walked two batters and hit another, a reporter actually asked him after the game, "Was this the worst stuff you've had in a game?"

"Imagine the pressure," Smoltz says, of knowing that, in every start for two years, if you give up two runs in a complete game your ERA is going to go *up*. But he has this way of constantly deflecting the attention and pressure off himself."

Back home in his basement den in suburban Atlanta a few days later, fueled by a pizza, a box of wings and a soda, Maddux is reviewing a videotape of his game against the Giants. He is harsher on himself than any of the reporters he sent away that day with his usual polite responses.

After giving up a leadoff double to Deion Sanders, Maddux retires the next six batters, on five grounders and a foul pop-up. And this is his comment after that stretch: "Right there I'm thinking I have to pitch better. I'm not going to be lucky all day."

He ends the third by getting Sanders on a fly ball to center field on a change-up that, Maddux says, "got a lot of the plate. I've got to get it away more the next time."

In the fifth, it becomes clear why he gave up one of his two walks on the day. There are two outs and a runner on second when Giants third baseman Steve Scarsone comes to bat. Maddux checks the San Francisco bullpen before pitching to Scarsone, the number 8 hitter. When he sees that no one is warming up, he knows that Giants manager Dusty Baker has to let his pitcher, Terry Mulholland, hit. He walks Scarsone on six pitches before dismissing Mulholland on three straight strikes.

The biggest out of the game is vintage Maddux. The Giants have the tying runs on base in the sixth with two outs and first baseman J.R. Phillips hitting. Maddux goes ahead 0 and 2, on three pitches down and away, the last being hit foul. So he comes knifing inside with one of those cutters, so far inside it almost hits Phillips' belly button. Still, Phillips swings and fouls it off.

The only way Phillips swings at a pitch like that, Maddux decides, is if he is looking for a pitch inside. So Maddux comes back with a change-up down and away, even though O'Brien, to further the deception, sets up inside. Phillips is fooled. He taps a weak bouncer to the right side. Maddux dives to stop it, then throws out Phillips from his knees with a backhand flip.

There is something else. Something Maddux figured out that made him sure Phillips would never expect that pitch. Something that Maddux does not want to reveal publicly.

His eyes light up, and he grins a silly grin. This is a man who is the master at undressing hitters while cloaking himself in camouflage. A magician never explains a trick. Let it remain, to our ceaseless amazement, part of the mystery of Maddux.

1995

E.M. Swift

∂⸱

From Bringing Up Junior

You kind of want to put the whole show under glass and preserve it forever, before it changes, the way people wanted to do when Willie Mays first came up and the Say Hey Kid won everybody's heart. Now there's *this* kid: Junior. It's more than just the breathtaking baseball skills you want to capture — his great arm, his fluid stride, his viperlike upper-cut swing. It's the whole darn affair: The 40-year-old father, in his 18th major-league season, catching a plane on a day off to watch his namesake make a dazzling over-the-wall catch that reminds everyone of a catch he, the father, made five years earlier in the very same stadium. The teammates on the Seattle Mariners who thrill to his exploits and bear him no jealousy. The nickname, Junior, and how he still calls home every night — collect — to tell his mother, Alberta, about the game. The pure joy that the kid derives from playing, which, on a good day, can be felt in the far corners of the stands. The way he turns this big-buck, high-pressure business called baseball back into a playground game.

You want to keep all that for posterity. But there is a problem. You also want to fast-forward the calendar so you can see Ken Griffey Jr. in his prime. You kind of want to find out just how great a player he will someday be when he actually gets serious about baseball. Not serious like Will Clark-serious, walking around with an I'm-looking-for-the-cure-for-cancer expression wrinkling his brow. Just, you know, serious. Like, paying attention to who's pitching. Learning the names of some of the opposing players, so he can position himself in the outfield. Watching relievers warm up before he faces them for the first time. Little things.

Unless, of course, that's the whole secret to the 20-year-old Griffey's success: that he doesn't unnecessarily complicate the fundamentally simple concept of hitting the ball with the bat and catching it with the glove. Hitting the bejesus out of the ball, as a matter of fact, as no 20-year-old player has hit it in the major leagues since Al Kaline batted .340 at that age to win the 1955 American League batting title. Making running catches with his back to the plate, which draws inescapable comparisons to Mays. And, as long as we're mentioning Hall of Famers, making throws from the outfield that are of the same general caliber as the cannon shots of Roberto Clemente. It's almost as if Griffey was born to do this kind of work.

And he's still the youngest player in the major leagues. Same as he was last year. That's the scary part. "People are comparing him to Jose Canseco," says Seattle pitcher Matt Young. "He's only 20 years old. Jose was 22 when he made it in the major leagues."

"He's a big kid, a baby," says Gene Clines, the Mariners' hitting coach. "When he finally buckles down and gets serious about this game, there's no telling what kind of numbers he will put on the board."

A big kid who, truth be told, is still growing. Everybody swears it, though the Mariners' media guide lists him this year at 6'3", 195, same as last. Griffey himself claims to have added "about two pounds," shrugging off observations that he seems to stand a full inch taller and that his chest, hips and thighs have all filled out. Says Clines, "I don't think anybody's ever been that good at that age. He's in his own category. He is a natural."

Capitalize that: a Natural. The kind of player after whom babies and candy bars are named.

Last Thursday night's game in Yankee Stadium can serve as a case in point. In a 6-2 Mariners win, Griffey went 2-for-4 and scored a run. Nothing new there. He hits to all fields with power and has been swinging a hot bat since spring training. As of Sunday he had hit in 13 of his last 14 games; he led the American League in hitting with a .395 average and was among the league leaders in hits (30), total bases (49), home runs (5) and RBIs (17).

But the play that had everyone buzzing, which even brought Yankee fans out of their seats, was a catch Griffey made on a ball hit by Jesse Barfield that robbed the Yankee right fielder (if only for a couple of innings, as it turned out) of his 200th career home run. Starting from his position in straightaway center, medium depth, Griffey took off toward the left-center field wall as Barfield's shot sailed into the night sky. Griffey hit the warning track full tilt, gauged the wall at a glance, and, like a long jumper marking his takeoff, sunk his cleat halfway up the foam padding on the wall and leapt. From the bullpen, which in Yankee Stadium is beyond the nearly eight-foot-high center field wall, the Mariners pitchers could see only an arm flying over the top, as if disembodied. Then the arm whiplashed back, out of sight, and the ball, which had appeared so briefly, vanished with it.

"As I jumped, I thought, I got a chance," Griffey said afterward, calling it the best catch he had ever made. "That's the first one I've caught going over the wall, in practice or in a game."

The catch was the third out of the inning; Griffey landed as if still in stride and headed for the dugout as part of a single continuous motion. He glanced over at Mariners left fielder Jeffrey Leonard, who threw his head back and rolled his eyes in disbelief. Griffey cracked up. He came sprinting back to the infield with the biggest grin anyone's seen in Yankee Stadium since Morgana was patrolling the place. When he got a look at Barfield standing between first and second with an angry expression on his face, Griffey cracked up again. "That's why I like playing defense," he says, "because it's the only time I get to see somebody else but me get mad."

In the stands a woman tapped Ken Griffey Sr. on the shoulder — it was just the third major-league game he had ever seen Junior play —and asked "Is that your son?"

Griffey Sr. nodded.

"Jesse Barfield's my husband," Maria Barfield said.

As Junior loped in, still grinning, the Yankee fans rose to applaud him, the Yankee brass upstairs got to their feet, and the Mariners poured onto the field to greet him with high fives. "He shared that catch with all of us," Seattle coach Julio Cruz said later. "It pumped us all up."

Everyone, friend and foe. It was one of those great baseball moments. The next time Barfield came to bat, he homered seven rows deep to right center, and as he crossed the plate he told Mariners catcher Scott Bradley, "If he'd caught that one, I'd have had his urine checked."

1990

Don DeLillo

From Pafko at the Wall

Peanut vendor's coming through
again, a coin-catching wiz about eighteen, black and rangy.
People know him from games past and innings gone and
they quicken up and dig for change. They're calling out for
peanuts, hey, here, yo, and tossing coins with thumb flicks
and discus arcs and in every known manner of hurled pro-
jectile, and the vendor's hands seem to inhale the flying metal.
He is magnet-skinned, snatching backhand and off his ear
and between his dang legs. People cheering him on and pea-
nut bags sailing left and right. The guy is Mr. Everything. He
circus-catches dimes they fling from ten rows away, then
airmails the peanuts to them chest-high.

1992

Steve Rushin
❧
From Ballpark Food

We came, we saw, we scarfed. We checked out the fare at all 28 major-league ballparks and judged their culinary offerings according to our home-cooked rating system: zero to four hot dogs, including halves.

ATLANTA BRAVES
Atlanta-Fulton County Stadium

Gotta Try: Eating before you get to the ballpark.

Avoid: The corn dog, an uncooked frank in a cornmeal condom.

Beer List: Includes Marthasville, described by one Atlantan as "popular with Southern women."

Ambiance: Muggy and buggy and smells like a urinal.

Rating: ½ hot dog

BALTIMORE ORIOLES
Oriole Park at Camden Yards

Gotta Try: The moist Maryland crabcake sandwiches, chased by a cinnamon-batter Uncle Teddy's hand-rolled soft pretzel.

Avoid: Too many glasses of the Orioles' unofficial drink, served in the bar of the Camden Club restaurant in the warehouse beyond right field: It's orange Stolichnaya.

Beer List: Extensive, which may explain the long line at the designated-driver sign-up booth.

Ambiance: On cobbled Eutaw Street beyond the right and center field bleachers are Boog's barbecue and Bambino's Ribs, a pair of CholesterAll-Stars.

Rating: 4 hot dogs

BOSTON RED SOX
Fenway Park

Gotta Try: The clam chowder from the Legal Seafood stand, behind the home plate box seats, has been described as "real thick, with lots of clams." Then again, so has Jose Canseco.

Avoid: The Bigbat pretzel. It's shaped like a bat, although it's not nearly as flavorful.

Beer List: Baseball under the lights: Amstel Light, Bud Light, Coors Light, Michelob Light, Miller Lite, and Rolling Rock Light.

Ambiance: To quote the beer maker, it doesn't get any better than this.

Rating: 3 hot dogs

CALIFORNIA ANGELS
Anaheim Stadium

Gotta Try: The cinnamon rolls, irredeemably unhealthful and spackled with frosting.

Avoid: Any of the many piscatory offerings, which include a variety of sushi. To be safe, don't even watch Angels outfielder Tim Salmon.

Beer List: Try the Corona with a wedge of lime for a quintessential SoCal experience.

Ambiance: Perhaps it's the beguiling cinnamon-roll scent, but something about the place makes people hungry. Years ago a plane buzzed the Big A trailing a banner advertising a local appearance by singer Jimmy Buffett. Angels third base coach Moose Stubing asked, "What's the big deal about Jimmy's buffet?"

Rating: 3 hot dogs

CHICAGO CUBS
Wrigley Field

Gotta Try: Smuggling in Char-Cheddar Dogs from the world-famous Wiener Circle, a hole-in-the-wall south of Wrigley on Clark Street.

Avoid: Concession-stand sausages, which haven't been the same since Smokey Links were dropped from the menu a few years ago.

Beer List: Old Style is the opium of the bleacher masses. So is Bud, endorsed by Harry Caray, one celebrity spokesman who clearly uses the product.
Ambiance: Ivied walls and frat-house clientele.
Rating: 2 hot dogs

CHICAGO WHITE SOX
Comiskey Park

Gotta Try: The peanut-butter-and-jelly sandwiches dispensed at the Kid's Corner counter, built chest-high to an eight-year-old, the better to embarrass you as you order.
Avoid: The pizza, which can't hold a coronary candle to the Chicago-style deep-dish pizzas served at Uno or Gino's downtown.
Beer List: As of mid-July, 12 brands will be served up at dat typical Chicago gaddering place: Da stadium sports bar.
Ambiance: Charm-free, like the dull brown exterior of the stadium itself.
Rating: 3 hot dogs

CINCINNATI REDS
Riverfront Stadium

Gotta Try: The Gold Star cheese coney, a hot dog buried in chili and shredded cheese. Cincinnati is, after all, Chili City.
Avoid: The one-dollar dog. Given the contents of a standard hot dog, the economy frank is too frightful to countenance.
Beer List: The best is Oldenberg Holy Grail Nut Brown Ale, brewed six miles away in Fort Mitchell, Ky. The worst is Hudy Delight, containing more bad hops than the Riverfront infield.
Ambiance: Only one smoking box in the joint, but it might be available soon.
Rating: 1 hot dog

CLEVELAND INDIANS
Jacobs Field

Gotta Try: Anything from the Calorie Gallery behind the first base stands, where a bakery offers giant cookies, cinnamon rolls, brownies, eclairs, etc. The Peterson Nut Company, across the street from the Jake, has the city's best nut never to have worn the number 8.
Avoid: Italian sausage sandwiches failed at the Jake. Are the black-peppercorn Polish sausage sandwiches any better?
Beer List: Three specialty kiosks serve 14 brands, including Cleveburg's own Great Lakes and Crooked River. Careful, the latter brand is flammable.

Ambiance: Baseball's most exclusive bistro. It's fully booked through the end of the season.
Rating: 4 hot dogs

COLORADO ROCKIES
Coors Fields

Gotta Try: The brisket-of-buffalo sandwich and, of course, the Rocky Mountain oysters.
Avoid: The Rocky Mountain oysters and, of course, the brisket-of-buffalo sandwich.
Beer List: Your choices are, admirably, not limited to the macrobrew with which the field shares its name: The on-site Sandlot Brewery is a malt meritocracy, and it does business even when the Rockies are away.
Ambiance: View of Rockies enhanced by view of Rockies. And vice versa.
Rating: 4 hot dogs

DETROIT TIGERS
Tiger Stadium

Gotta Try: The frozen daiquiris, which render the Tigers almost watchable. The barbecued ribs, says one fan, "slide right off the bone, just like they should."
Avoid: Little Caesars pizza, on principle: The chain is owned by Mike Ilitch, who is also the proprietor of baseball's worst team.
Beer List: Twenty varieties, from Molson Golden to Molson Canadian to Molson Ice.
Ambiance: The Tigers are the best appetite suppressant in the big leagues.
Rating: 3 hot dogs

FLORIDA MARLINS
Joe Robbie Stadium

Gotta Try: Bru's Wings, the chicken wings cooked up by former Dolphins bruiser Bob Brudzinski. They're finger-breakin' good.
Avoid: The rabid corn dogs.
Beer List: The Port of Call stand carries 24 brands, including Southpaw Light, one left-handed pitcher you'll be happy to send down.
Ambiance: With Caribbean mojo chicken, Cuban sandwiches, *arepas* (Venezuelan flat grilled corn-flour muffins with mozzarella filling) and paella, the Marlins are Latin America's team.
Rating: 3½ hot dogs

HOUSTON ASTROS
Astrodome

Gotta Try: The footlong jalapeño sausage on a stick. It's so greasy that the stick is a dipstick. Doctors at the concessions counter conveniently schedule the next day's angioplasty.

Avoid: The Lone Star burger. Dry. Unmoist. An arid, unirrigated testament to cheeseburger dehydration.

Beer List: The Bud Light, Miller Lite, Coors Light, Bud and Red Dog are poured ice-cold from 16-ounce cans. Texas-brewed Shiner Bock is available in 12-ounce bottles only. The Bud Light on tap tastes as if the keg has not been changed since the '86 playoffs.

Ambiance: Slightly above the caves of Cro-Magnon man and oddly devoid of regional influences. There is no seafood and no shrimp save for John Cangelosi.

Rating: 2 hot dogs

KANSAS CITY ROYALS
Kauffman Stadium

Gotta Try: The "grilled pretzels, charcoal-baked" if only to learn what a grilled, baked product tastes like.

Avoid: Popcorn. The Royals have added four new poppers this year, but this is still the worst maize since Willie's final season, with the Mets in '73.

Beer List: Includes Zima. 'Nuff said?

Ambiance: Kansas City is famous for its barbecue, so the poor quality of the ballpark's is conspicuous.

Rating: 2½ hot dogs

LOS ANGELES DODGERS
Dodger Stadium

Gotta Try: The long, lean Dodger Dog, which costs $2.50 and is available at 44 stands. There was a near riot in 1991 when, briefly, the dogs were steamed rather than grilled. Fans were steamed, and the vendors were grilled — and soon the hot dogs were returned to the Weber. Have a Cool-a-Coo ice-cream sandwich for dessert, and thank us later.

Avoid: The Yoshinoya Beef Bowl, which isn't the new title sponsor of the Rose Bowl but rather an L.A. fast-foot Japanese restaurant whose stand is inexplicably popular at Dodger Stadium. The "beef" in the Beef Bowl — served on a bed of rice, complete with chopsticks — consists of limp strips of what looks like uncooked bacon. Grisly and gristly.

Beer List: Includes Sapporo, the better to wash down the sushi (10 pieces for $5.25) sold by vendors in what Aramark

general manager Lon Rosenberg calls "traditional Japanese garb." Says Rosenberg of the sushi: "It does really well when Hideo Nomo is pitching."
Ambiance: May be baseball's most beautiful setting.
Rating: 3 hot dogs

MILWAUKEE BREWERS
County Stadium

Gotta Try: Gas-grilled bratwurst dressed in Sportservice's Secret Stadium Sauce, a beguiling, spicy red condiment somewhere between ketchup and barbecue sauce. Especially good to tuck into while watching the nightly scoreboard races, which pit three animated sausages against one another.
Avoid: The salted, buttered popcorn, which will make the first number in your blood-pressure reading resemble Ted Williams' lifetime average.
Beer List: Miller-intensive, to be sure, but the acclaimed Leinenkugel's ("Leiney's" to cheeseheads) is also available.
Ambiance: It's all in the County Stadium parking lot, the best tailgating site in sports. "If you didn't have tailgating," says Sportservice general manager Tom Olson, "there wouldn't be nearly so many people here."
Rating: 3 hot dogs

MINNESOTA TWINS
Metrodome

Gotta Try: The Jumbo Dog, baseball's biggest. More than a meal, it's a double-bypass in a bun.
Avoid: The paper cup filled with plastic-foam-packing peanuts. Sorry, that's the popcorn.
Beer List: Grain Belt, an award-winning brew named for the lowest rank in all of karate.
Ambiance: It's so lacking that this season the Twins opened an alfresco pregame gathering place across the street.
Rating: 1½ hot dogs

MONTREAL EXPOS
Olympic Stadium

Gotta Try: The ribs at Rusty 10, an in-house restaurant named for ex-'Po Rusty Staub. Team president Claude Brochu imported the recipe from Park Ave. BBQ & Grill, his favorite joint near the Expos' spring training complex in West Palm Beach.
Avoid: Place Tevère in the Stade Olympique. It offers the unctuous oxymoron that is French pizza. Also think twice about the "catcher's gloves," described by Sportservice as

"puffed dough in the shape of a catcher's glove, with a base-ball" etched on the palm. The glove is stuffed with spicy Tex-Mex filling, pork sausage or ground chicken, but the ball does not, as of yet, have a cushioned-cork center.

Beer List: Canadian national brands, some of which have a higher alcohol content than U.S. beers.

Ambiance: Induces what the French call *ennui*.

Rating: 2 hot dogs

NEW YORK METS

Shea Stadium

Gotta Try: Carolina Barbecue Co. in right field does commendable beef, pork, and turkey sandwiches on a steak roll, in sauce the makers claim is "soon to be famous." But don't hold your breath. Better yet, after eating this, do hold your breath.

Avoid: The Buffalo Mild sauce that comes with the Chicken Tenders and Wow Wings. Neon orange and watery, it suspiciously matches the field-level seat paint.

Beer List: Microbrew carts dispense two New Amsterdam varieties: Amber and Blonde, apparently named for Mets groupies.

Ambiance: You'll get buzzed, if only by airplanes landing at adjacent La Guardia.

Rating: 2 hot dogs

NEW YORK YANKEES

Yankee Stadium

Gotta Try: The sweet Italian sausage, which is not made from Phil Rizzuto.

Avoid: The Pastrami-Seasoned Turkey Sandwich. This is a Sybil of a sandwich built around a cold cut with an identity crisis. Is it pastrami or is it turkey? You make the call.

Beer List: Among the microbrews are Rhino Chaser and Old Thumper. Have you noticed? Beers now have better names than ballplayers.

Ambiance: SoHo prices, SoBro locale.

Rating: 4 hot dogs

OAKLAND ATHLETICS

Oakland Coliseum

Gotta Try: Hot links from Oaktown's famous Everett & Jones Barbecue. The extrahot induces eyelid sweat. East Bay's Your Black Muslim Bakery claims to sell an "all-natural cinnamon roll," which is like finding an all-natural Baywatch actress.

Avoid: The nuclear nachos.

Beer List: Order a Widmer-Hefeweizen, and prepare to hear your server say, "Gesundheit."

Ambiance: Also, Al Davis is the maitre d', but vibrations from the constant construction jackhammering do aid the digestive process.

Rating: 3 hot dogs

PHILADELPHIA PHILLIES
Veterans Stadium

Gotta Try: The Phillie Phanatic uses an ingenious hot dog launcher to strafe fans with frankfire. Snag a wrapped wiener, wash it down with a Rita's Water Ice.

Avoid: The Superpretzels. In a city rightly famous for its soft pretzels, some customers say the Vet's taste as if they were defrosted and guess they were frozen about the time Walt Disney was. Instead, on your way to the park, get some pretzels fresh from the oven at the Federal Pretzel Banking Company in South Philly.

Beer List: There are 28 brands, priced from $4.75 for domestic drafts to a landmark $8 for Anchor Steam. Alas, the Phanatic does not yet douse the crowd with a beer cannon.

Ambiance: Penitentiarylike, except at the stadium restaurant in right field. It has sit-down tables but this disadvantage: There's a view of the field and, thus, the Phillies.

Rating: 2 hot dogs

PITTSBURGH PIRATES
Three Rivers Stadium

Gotta Try: Primanti's Pittsburgh-style cheesesteak, a hamburger patty topped with cheese, slaw and fries, all jammed between two slices of Italian bread. True 'burghers douse it with Louisiana hot sauce.

Avoid: Sitting near anyone who has eaten the above.

Beer List: Iron City and Penn Pilsner, the latter sold thanks to new Pirates owner Kevin McClatchy.

Ambiance: It's only found in the barbecue tent outside gate A.

Rating: 2 hot-dogs

SAN DIEGO PADRES
Jack Murphy Stadium

Gotta Try: Rubio's fish tacos, the equal of any served in Tijuana. Also, former Cy Young Award winner Randy Jones makes a wildly popular chicken dish called Fowl Territory — and actually chats with customers while serving it.

Avoid: The sweet tamale, stuffed with pineapple and cinnamon. Foul territory indeed.

Beer List: Bud and Miller dominate in this puritanical park, where alcohol is available only at food stands and beer is not available in the Padres' clubhouse. This is, of course, sacrilege in a stadium named for a sportswriter.

Ambiance: Laid-back, back, back, back, back.

Rating: 2 hot dogs

SAN FRANCISCO GIANTS

3Com Park

Gotta Try: The Stinking Rose 40-Clove Garlic Chicken Sandwich and garlic french fries. "Bad for the breath and bad for the diet," raves Don Solem, a Giant season-ticket holder who is fast becoming a giant season-ticket holder.

Avoid: The tofu dog, the color and texture of a pencil eraser.

Beer List: Twenty premium bottled brands, though the coldest draft is still the one that blows in off the bay.

Ambiance: Haute cuisine served in a charmless dump, which is the equivalent of Chardonnay decanted into plastic cups (something they actually offer here).

Rating: 4 hot dogs

SEATTLE MARINERS

KingDome

Gotta Try: The nachos, which are so popular that they have their own stands. Alas, the lines flow as slowly as the "cheez."

Avoid: Drinking soda. In March The *Seattle Times* reported that last fall a stand worker had seen a colleague use an ice shovel to scoop up garbage, then ice.

Beer List: Red Hook is a popular local brand, though Starbucks is still the city's favorite brew.

Ambiance: A concrete crypt in which smokers are envied: They get to hang out on the open-air concourses and stare out at Puget Sound.

Rating: 1 hot dog

ST. LOUIS CARDINALS

Busch Stadium

Gotta Try: The Missouri courts gotta try whoever recently removed toasted ravioli from the menu. It's a ballpark delicacy that was available only at Busch. What were they thinking?

Avoid: Ordering beer after the seventh inning, when they sell only O'Doul's.

Beer List: Anheuser-Busch has sold the team but still holds a bland-beer near monopoly in the stadium.

Ambiance: So clean you could eat off the floor, though nobody has since the Phillies last left town.
Rating: 2½ hot dogs

TEXAS RANGERS
The Ballpark in Arlington

Gotta Try: The Authentic Texas Barbecue, which is available throughout the stadium. Beef brisket, baby-back ribs, and chicken are smoked to sticky perfection on the Ballpark's $25,000 smoker which can handle 700 pounds of meat at a single cooking.

Avoid: The Italian sausage. It's dry and lumpy and caused one diner to conclude that he had "found Jimmy Hoffa."

Beer List: In a welcome innovation, the Ballpark cycles 10 new premium beers through its gourmet brew stands each month so that fans can in turn cycle the beers through themselves.

Ambiance: Overwhelmingly friendly service in a gorgeous setting. Alas, unbearable blast-furnace heat arrives by late July.

Rating: 4 hot dogs

TORONTO BLUE JAYS
SkyDome

Gotta Try: Bavarian Beer Nuts (Oddly enough, this was the original name of the Nazi party.)

Avoid: Yogen-Früz. Is it delicious yogurt or is it a Swedish skin condition?

Beer List: The Hard Rock Cafe in right field serves Moosehead. Bring along some Woodpecker cider and mix it with the beer to create an exceptional Moosepecker. In the rest of the park, there is Labatt's Blue, Labatt's Blue Light, Labatt's Classic, Labatt's Old Mix, Labatt's Ice...wait a minute: Who owns the Blue Jays?

Ambiance: As ex-Jay Lloyd Moseby once noted, the entire stadium is a shopping-mall food court.

Rating: 3 hot dogs

1996

Roger Angell

❧

From Fans ♥ Yanks

The weather for last week's ticker tape parade, celebrating the Yankees' unexpected World Championship and even more unlikely emergence as national sweetie pies, was perfect: deep blue skies; a tingly, post-baseball snap to the air; a midday blizzard downtown. With the crime rate down, the Dow Jones over six thousand, Frank Torre's new heart thumping away, and Jeff Maier supplanting Madonna's baby as Junior Icon, everything has been getting so nice in New York that it feels like Topeka around here. Winning big isn't exactly new for the Apple, to be sure: with nine major-sport franchises in the local loop, these championship celebrations (for the New Jersey Devils last year, for the Rangers in 1994, for the football Giants in 1991) should no longer take us by surprise. What was different about the three-million turnout last Tuesday was the makeup of this particular Yankee team, each of its members now waving and beaming from those raised floats that have replaced Grover Whalen's shiny black touring cars, and the

look on the faces of their surging, Macarena-writhing, jump-
ing-in-the-air fans. Out of uniform now, the passing heroes
— Derek Jeter in black leather and killer shades, Cecil Fielder
with a video camera and a fat cigar, Wade Boggs in a fetch-
ing, perhaps faux, squirrel coat — looked younger than they
ever did in the on-deck circle; most of all, they looked relieved. Never mind triumph — this was about happiness.

For late-season watchers, baseball's clock-free, pitch-by-
pitch disclosures and its fondness for startling changes of
mood and theme from one game to the next (the Yankees' 8-
6 comeback from a six-run deficit in the fourth Series game
took four hours and seventeen minutes; the next night's edgy,
masterly 1-0 shutout by Andy Pettitte was over almost before the eleven-o'clock news) accumulate a complexity of
emotion and possibility that is probably beyond the reach of
other sports. Luck and skill (and boredom) show their faces
by turns, and impending disaster, frustrated hopes, renewed
anxiety, and recurrent sudden release can contribute to an
almost insupportable sense of strain. Baseball feels like life
sometimes, and when, contrary to experience, all goes well
out there — remember Charlie Hayes' tiny roller that stayed
fair down the third-base line; remember Paul O'Neill gimpily
sprinting after and then catching up to that deep drive for a
last out — we feel an end-of-the-day sort of satisfaction that
is deeper than any "We're Number One!" exultation. Next
morning, when the game comes flooding back to mind, the
unlikelihood of it is what makes us smile.

Those 1996 Yankees are nothing like the 1986 Mets —
the Keith Hernandez, Gary Carter, Lenny Dykstra, Wally
Backman champions, whose on-the-field high-fiving, off-the-
field carousing, and coolly sophisticated maneuverings of
the media made them hated in the heartland, even after they
captured the amazing Sixth Game and went on to confirm

the Red Sox's worst fears about themselves. What we felt for them here in town was a raging ironic pride. This is New York, America, and up yours. What we feel now is that we're Jimmy Stewart. We want to go out and hug somebody, preferably another relative or friend of Joe Torre's. If the Bronxian postseason looked more and more like a Capra script as it wound down, the manager was Oscar-worthy character-role casting. Saturnine, worn, and baggy-faced, with those water-spaniel eyes and candy-stained lips, this Brooklyn-born Joe was a dad for all seasons. The engaging diversity of his players was movielike as well: a tall, shy, classical-guitar-playing star center fielder in Bernie Williams; the cheerfully self-assured rookie shortstop Derek Jeter; the slick-smooth, late-flame-throwing Mariano Rivera; the Roman-beaked lefty ace Andy Pettitte; the surgically restored, palely staring David Cone; the gentle, bus-size slugger Cecil Fielder; and so on. Darryl Strawberry and Doc Gooden had been celebrity Mets a decade ago. Here, with the Yankees, they were less and also more: diminished heroes now in recovery, with a grateful look about them for the chance of each new day. Paul O'Neill, Jim Leyritz, John Wetteland, Tino Martinez, Mariano Duncan, and Wade Boggs were highly paid, robust veterans, alike in their resolute skills and absence of pout. What these players and the other Yankees held in common was open respect for their manager, and that, too, feels scripted and old-style in 1996. Even the owner was different this time around — less Georgian, for a change; almost deblustered.

None of this will last long. Next year's Yankees will be even richer, and they will grow wary of the insatiable media swarm that feeds on champions. Some of the young Yanks will become more familiar to us in TV commercials, where the qualities that made them feel so fresh will be morphed into sentimentality or worn to parody by endless repetition.

Some of their old teammates will be playing elsewhere. Once the season starts, the games will be harder and less fun, with the burden of repeating almost visible above the field with every pitch, every play. We Yankee fans will be more critical, now that we know what to expect, and when our guys fall on their faces out there, as all ballplayers do, we'll boo. Fans around the country will feel free to begin hating the Yankees once again. Maybe this won't be such a bad thing. Do we in New York want to go around looking like a bunch of wimpy smilers and huggers for a whole year? Do we want to be happy every day? Naah.

1996

THOMAS BOSWELL is a syndicated sports columnist for the *Washington Post*. He is the author of *Strokes of Genius*, *The Heart of the Order*, and *Cracking the Show*.

Excerpt from *Cracking the Show* copyright 1994 by Thomas Boswell. Reprinted by permission of Bantam Doubleday Dell Publishing Group, Inc.

JIMMY BRESLIN is the author of *World Without End, Amen*, *Table Money*, and most recently, *I Want to Thank my Brain for Remembering Me*. He won the Pulitzer Prize in 1986.

Excerpt from *Can't Anybody Here Play This Game* copyright 1963 by Jimmy Breslin. Reprinted by permission.

PETER COHEN wrote one novel, *Diary of a Simple Man*.

Excerpt from *Diary of a Simple Man* copyright 1961 by Peter Cohen.

MARK GALLAGHER, PAUL SUSMAN, AND ROBERT SCHIEWE combined to produce *Explosion: The Legendary Home Runs of Mickey Mantle*.

Excerpt from *Explosion: The Legendary Home Runs of Mickey Mantle* copyright 1987 by Mark Gallagher, Paul Susman, and Robert Schiewe. Reprinted by permission.

ARTHUR DALEY wrote sports for *The Times* for forty-seven years and won a Pulitzer Prize.

Excerpt from *The Arthur Daley Years* copyright 1975 by Arthur Daley. Reprinted by permission of Quadrangle, The New York Times Book Co.

DAVID HALBERSTAM is the author of such books as *The Best and the Brightest*, *The Breaks of the Game*, and *October 1964*.

Excerpt from *The Summer of '49* copyright 1989 by David Halberstam. Reprinted by permission of William Morrow and Co.

W.C. HEINZ was a war correspondent and sports writer, and author of *Run to Daylight!* (with Vince Lombardi) and *The Professional*.